THE OFFICIAL GUIDE TO

PTE ACADEMIC™

PEARSON TEST OF ENGLISH ACADEMIC

FROM THE TEST DEVELOPERS

Pearson Education Limited
Edinburgh Gate
Harlow
Essex CM20 2JE
England
and Associated Companies throughout the world.

www.pearsonelt.com

Licensed edition from the Pearson Education Asia edition, entitled *The Official Guide to PTE Pearson Test of English* Academic published by Pearson Longman Asia ELT Copyright © 2010.

First published 2010
This edition published 2012

ISBN: 978-1-4479-2891-1

Sixth Impression 2016

Set in 11.5/14pt Minion
Printed in Malaysia, CTP-PJB

Acknowledgements
The publishers would like to thank the following people and institutions for their feedback and comments during the development of the material:

From **Second Language Test, Inc**
Lauren Kennedy (Director, Test Development) and Catherine Casteel (Test Developer and Literacy Specialist) for writing and revising the Overview and Task sections in Chapters 3-6
Corinna Duron (Test Developer) for reviewing the Overview and Task sections in Chapters 3-6

Margaret Matthews (Writer and editor, educational materials) for writing and reviewing the Test preparation guidelines section in Chapter 1 and the strategies sections in Chapters 3-6
Betty Jean Gran (Consultant, Training and Development Services) for writing the general skills sections in Chapters 3-6

Alison Ross (PTE Academic reviewer) for reviewing the CD-ROM practice items

SunMi Ma and her Reading Comprehension class, Vikki Weston, Mandy Evans, Nisreen Hasan, Chris Baker, Mark Knight, Christopher Fulton and Varisara Payananol for reviewing the *Official Guide* and providing valuable insights and suggestions

Contents

Introduction to the *Official Guide*

Pearson Test of English Academic (PTE Academic) is an international computer-based English language test. It provides a measure of test takers' language ability to education institutions, and professional and government organizations that require a standard of academic English for admission purposes.

The Official Guide to PTE Academic is designed for anyone who wants to prepare for PTE Academic or learn more about the test. The guide, along with its companion Audio CD and CD-ROM, will help you:

- find out how to register for PTE Academic
- understand the features, format and scoring
- learn how to respond to each item type
- become familiar with the language skills assessed
- practice answering authentic test items
- improve your test-taking strategies

What is in the guide?

Main chapters

The guide includes six chapters.

Chapter 1 provides an overview of PTE Academic, including a description of **key features**, **format** and **scoring**. Chapter 2 offers general **test preparation guidelines**, and lists **other resources** to supplement the practice in the *Official Guide*. This chapter also includes information about what to expect **on the test day**.

Chapters 3–6 are divided by skill and cover the 20 item types found in PTE Academic and the skills assessed in each case. The item types are presented in the same order as in the test. Chapter 3 introduces the **five speaking item types**, Chapter 4 the **two writing item types**, Chapter 5 the **five reading item types** and Chapter 6 the **eight listening item types**.

In Chapters 3–6, discussion of each item type begins with a task item to help you become familiar with the **on-screen appearance** of the different parts of the actual test. Explanations of the **scoring** follow to help you understand which factors within your response to each item type are scored and which language skills are tested. **Test-taking strategies** outline steps to improve your performance on each item type.

Finally, a **practice item** is presented, allowing you to apply what you have learned.

Some item types are individually timed. When you see the timer icon **15 sec.** in a practice item, be sure to time yourself as you answer the item.

Extra tips about PTE Academic and the *Official Guide* are provided in note boxes like this one.

Each chapter concludes with a **general skills section** outlining key areas of the communicative skills needed in everyday and test situations. A checklist for skills assessment is included to help you understand your strengths and weaknesses. Practice activities and strategies for helping you develop each communicative skill are suggested.

Answer key, glossary and appendices

The guide also includes an answer key and transcripts, a glossary and an appendix.

The Answer key provides **correct answers** and/or **sample responses** to the task and practice items included in Chapters 3–6. These sample responses are authentic responses given by test takers who took the PTE Academic pilot tests.

- PTE Academic was piloted with more than 10,000 test takers in 21 countries, including China, Japan, India, Australia and the United States.
- These test takers were born in 158 different countries speaking 126 different languages. They were university students having a similar level of English proficiency to that of the prospective PTE Academic test takers. A number of native speakers of English were also recruited as a control group.

Explanations about the correct answers for some practice items are also included.

When you see the Answer key icon Answer key p.165 , check your answer in the Answer key.

The Glossary provides brief **definitions** for the terms specific to PTE Academic and/or language testing.

The Appendix includes information about the **alignment of PTE Academic scores** to the levels of the Common European Framework of Reference for Languages (CEF or CEFR) and the CEF language descriptors.

What is on the Audio CD?

The Audio CD includes the **audio recordings** for the listening and speaking items, and **sample responses** for the speaking items presented in Chapters 3–6 of this guide.

When you see the CD icon in the guide, play the specified track on the Audio CD.

The three sample responses provided for each speaking item are authentic responses given by PTE Academic test takers. These responses illustrate the CEF levels of competence C1, B2 and B1. See the Appendix for information on the CEF language descriptors.

Use a voice recorder to record your spoken responses and compare them with these sample responses.

How to use the guide and the Audio CD

The *Official Guide* and the Audio CD include authentic test items taken from the PTE Academic test item bank. To get the most out of the test materials, we recommend that you follow these steps:

- Work through each task and follow the step-by-step information about each item type.
- Study the scoring information and pay particular attention to the language skills and test-taking strategies.
- Do the practice item at the end of each item type section. Try to simulate the conditions and time pressure of PTE Academic. For example, allow yourself the exact time specified for each task.
- Play the Audio CD to listen to the recordings for the listening and speaking items. Play the recordings only once during the practice.
- Use the Answer key to check your responses. Read the explanations and compare your written responses with the authentic sample responses given by PTE Academic test takers rated at the CEF levels C1, B2 and B1.
- Record your responses to the speaking items and compare them with the authentic sample responses on the Audio CD.

What is on the CD-ROM?

The CD-ROM is an interactive program containing over 200 additional practice items, written specifically to accompany the *Official Guide* and help you prepare for PTE Academic. The items included on the CD-ROM amount to three unscored tests. They are presented and responded to in a similar way to the actual test.

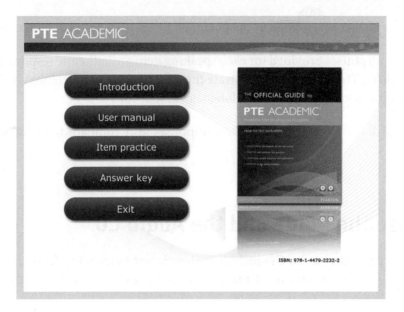

The Introduction describes the **content** of the CD-ROM and recommends **hints for study and practice** of the CD-ROM test items.

The User manual explains the CD-ROM **interface features** and **functionality**. It provides general information and instructions on **operating the CD-ROM software**.

The Item practice includes **three unscored practice sets** with a combination of items covering each of the language skills—speaking, writing, reading and listening—assessed in PTE Academic.

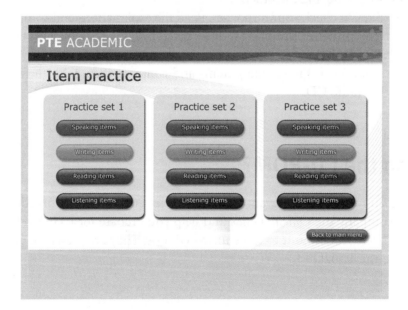

The table below describes the contents of the **Item practice** on the CD-ROM.

Skills group	Practice set 1 (number of items)	Practice set 2 (number of items)	Practice set 3 (number of items)
Speaking items	40	41	41
Writing items	3	4	4
Reading items	16	15	17
Listening items	20	19	17

In the Answer key you can view or play back **your responses** and compare them with the **sample responses** given by native speakers of English. You can read the **explanations** about why the response options are correct or incorrect, or why the sample essays are good responses.

The Answer key will help you understand the answers and learn how to respond to the items. It will also help you evaluate your performance and assess your progress.

PTE Academic

Introduction

Overview

The ability to communicate effectively in English is crucial to academic success for university and college students in an English-speaking environment. The purpose of Pearson Test of English Academic (PTE Academic) is to accurately assess the listening, reading, speaking and writing ability of test takers who want to study at institutions where English is the principal language of instruction.

If you are a non-native speaker of English and need to demonstrate your academic English language ability, PTE Academic is the test for you. The test provides an accurate measure of a test taker's English language proficiency to ensure success in courses and active participation in university and college-level education where English is the language of instruction. Institutions will use the results of PTE Academic to determine the actual English language skills of applicants when making admission decisions.

The Language Testing division of Pearson, the world's leading education company, is responsible for the development of PTE Academic. Test development professionals involved in producing the test are based in several countries, including the United States, the United Kingdom and Australia.

PTE Academic has been developed in accordance with the Council of Europe's Common European Framework of Reference (CEF or CEFR; Council of Europe, 2001), which is a widely accepted standard of ability or performance in language testing. Test items are also internationally approved to ensure that the test is representative of and measures international academic English.

Key features

Integrated skills items

As language skills do not occur in isolation, PTE Academic uses a variety of integrated skills item types to reveal how well you can use English language for oral and written communication. Integrated skills items are important for assessing English language proficiency because, in an academic environment, students are often required to combine several language skills to perform a task, for example, listening to or reading information and then responding orally.

PTE Academic test items are task-based, representing the range of functions and situations that you will encounter during academic studies in an English-speaking environment. For example, one item type asks you to demonstrate your understanding of a passage by providing a written summary, while another assesses your understanding of a lecture by asking you to retell the lecture. A different item type tests your ability to orally describe graphical information.

PTE Academic features 20 different item types, each assessing one language skill or a combination of language skills. Chapters 3–6 of the *Official Guide* describe each item type in terms of format, timing, expected response length and scoring criteria, and offer strategies to help you complete each item type.

Source materials

PTE Academic is designed to be representative of academic language demands within a university or college setting. Source materials used in PTE Academic are taken from real-life situations in an academic environment.

Reading texts

As a student at university and college level, you need to do a lot of skimming, scanning and critical reading to complete academic coursework and deal with campus situations. PTE Academic focuses on reading tasks across a wide range of topics and academic disciplines.

Reading texts used in PTE Academic include those of academic interest and those related to aspects of student life. Texts of academic interest include historical biographies and narratives, academic articles, book reviews, commentaries, editorials, critical essays, science reports and summaries, journal articles and scientific articles written for a general academic audience. Academic disciplines include arts, science, social studies, humanities, economics, business administration and more. You are not expected to have any prior knowledge of these academic disciplines. The test assesses your ability to comprehend information provided in a given text. Texts related to student life include instructions, course outlines, grant applications, notices, timetables and accommodation guides. Academic reading texts may be accompanied by graphic information.

Reading texts are taken from published sources, such as textbooks or websites containing useful information for academic audiences.

Introduction

Audio recordings

Audio recordings include characteristics of actual speech, such as accents and dialects, fillers, hesitations, false starts, self corrections and variations in delivery speed. In academic settings, it is important that you understand a wide variety of spoken language across different situations. You need to follow different modes of lectures such as audio, video and audiovisual, despite differences in accent and delivery speed.

Recordings used in PTE Academic include audio recordings of academic interest and those related to aspects of student life. Recordings of academic interest include lectures, presentations, discussions, interviews, debates and speeches appropriate for a general academic audience. Academic disciplines include arts, science, social studies, humanities, economics, business administration and more. You are not expected to have any prior knowledge of these academic disciplines. The test assesses your ability to comprehend information provided in a given recording. Recordings related to student life include instructions, announcements and notices. A recording may be accompanied by visuals such as a presentation slide, providing information about the setting and clues about where the language is being used. Video recordings may also be included.

Recordings are taken from sources such as websites containing useful information for students, or based on actual speech samples from universities and colleges.

Test delivery

PTE Academic is a computer-based test that is delivered through Pearson's secure network of test centers. For a list of test center locations, refer to the Pearson website at www.pearsonpte.com.

You can register for PTE Academic online at www.pearsonpte.com and schedule your test at a time convenient for you. When you register, you will create a secure web account with a unique user name and password. Please refer to "Registration and scheduling" in Chapter 2 for detailed information.

Accessing your score report

After taking the test, you will be notified by email when your PTE Academic scores are available (normally within five business days from your test date). Using your account, you will be able to view your scores and send them to institutions of your choice (up to seven selections per test order). For further guidance on accessing your test results, please refer to the *Test Taker Handbook* available at www.pearsonpte.com.

Your test results will be presented in a score report. Please refer to "Scoring" in this chapter for details about the PTE Academic score report. Your test scores will be valid for up to two years from your test date. After two years your scores will no longer be valid.

Retaking the test

You can take the test as often as you wish, but you can only schedule one test at a time. Subsequent tests may be scheduled immediately after you receive your scores. If you take the test more than once, you can select which score to send to an institution. For further information, please refer to the *Test Taker Handbook* available at www.pearsonpte.com.

Structure

PTE Academic assesses all four language skills—listening, reading, speaking and writing. The test will last approximately three hours. This includes an untimed introduction to the test and one optional break of up to 10 minutes.

PTE Academic consists of three main parts. You will receive a general introduction to the test and specific instructions about what to expect in each part of the test. Each part may contain a number of sections. Each section is individually timed. The table below shows the test structure.

Part of test	Section	Item type	Time allowed
Introduction			not timed
Part 1: Speaking and writing	Section 1	Personal introduction	1 minute
	Section 2	Read aloud	30–35 minutes
		Repeat sentence	
		Describe image	
		Re-tell lecture	
		Answer short question	
	Sections 3–4	Summarize written text	20 minutes
	Section 5	Summarize written text or Write essay	10 or 20 minutes
	Section 6	Write essay	20 minutes
Part 2: Reading		Multiple-choice, choose single answer	32–41 minutes
		Multiple-choice, choose multiple answers	
		Re-order paragraphs	
		Reading: Fill in the blanks	
		Reading & writing: Fill in the blanks	

Part of test	Section	Item type	Time allowed
Part 3: Listening	Section 1	Summarize spoken text	20 or 30 minutes
	Section 2	Multiple-choice, choose multiple answers	23–28 minutes
		Fill in the blanks	
		Highlight correct summary	
		Multiple-choice, choose single answer	
		Select missing word	
		Highlight incorrect words	
		Write from dictation	

Part 1: Speaking and writing

In Part 1 you will be tested on your speaking and writing skills. You will have approximately 77–93 minutes to complete this part. The table below shows the speaking and writing part of the test.

Part 1: Speaking and writing		
Section	Item type	Time allowed
Section 1	Personal introduction	1 minute
Section 2	Read aloud	30–35 minutes
	Repeat sentence	
	Describe image	
	Re-tell lecture	
	Answer short question	
Sections 3–4	Summarize written text	20 minutes
Section 5	Summarize written text or Write essay	10 or 20 minutes
Section 6	Write essay	20 minutes

The minimum and maximum timings indicated for the sections in the speaking and writing part of PTE Academic do not add up to the total minimum and maximum times stated for this part of the test (77–93 minutes). This is because different versions of the test are balanced for total length. No test taker will get the maximum or minimum times indicated on all sections.

PTE Academic is an integrated skills test. Some item types in this part of the test also assess reading and listening skills.

Section 1

In Section 1, before starting the scored part of the test, you will be asked to orally introduce yourself. You are not assessed on your performance in the Personal introduction section. Your response offers an additional security measure for institutions and provides some impression of you as a person to university admission officers. Your response will be sent together with your score report to the institutions you select.

You could talk about one or more of the following:

- your interests
- your plans for future study
- why you want to study abroad
- why you need to learn English
- why you chose PTE Academic

You will have 25 seconds to read the prompt and 30 seconds to record your response. The recording status box on screen will let you know when to start recording and when to complete your response. You must reply in your own words, as naturally as possible. You will not be able to re-record your response, so make sure you are ready to speak. The image below shows the Personal introduction section of the test.

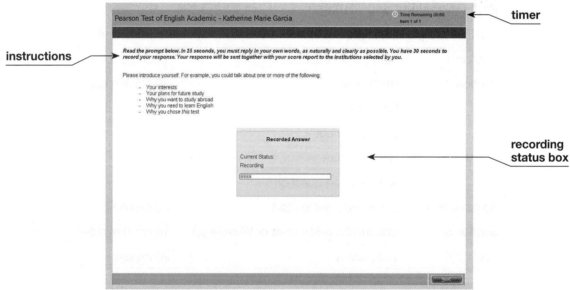

PTE Academic: Personal introduction section

Section 2

In Section 2, there is a single timed speaking section consisting of 35–42 independent and integrated skills items, depending on the combination of items in a given test. You will have approximately 30–35 minutes to complete this section. Different response formats are used in the speaking part of PTE Academic.

Sections 3–6

In Sections 3–6, there are three to four writing tasks, depending on the combination of items in a given test. Each task is in an individually timed section. Different response formats are used in the writing part of PTE Academic.

Part 2: Reading

In Part 2 you will be tested on your reading skills. You will have approximately 32–41 minutes to complete this part. The table below shows the reading part of the test.

Part 2: Reading	
Item type	Time allowed
Multiple-choice, choose single answer	32–41 minutes
Multiple-choice, choose multiple answers	
Re-order paragraphs	
Reading: Fill in the blanks	
Reading & writing: Fill in the blanks	

This is a single timed part containing 15–20 independent and integrated skills items, depending on the combination of items in a given test. Different response formats are used in the reading part of PTE Academic.

PTE Academic is an integrated skills test. One item type in this part of the test also assesses writing skills.

Part 3: Listening

In Part 3 you will be tested on your listening skills. You will have approximately 45–57 minutes to complete this part. The table below shows the listening part of the test.

Part 3: Listening

Section	Item type	Time allowed
Section 1	Summarize spoken text	20–30 minutes
Section 2	Multiple-choice, choose multiple answers	23–28 minutes
	Fill in the blanks	
	Highlight correct summary	
	Multiple-choice, choose single answer	
	Select missing word	
	Highlight incorrect words	
	Write from dictation	

> The minimum and maximum timings indicated for the sections in the listening part of PTE Academic do not add up to the total minimum and maximum times stated for this part of the test (45–57 minutes). This is because different versions of the test are balanced for total length. No test taker will get the maximum or minimum times indicated on all sections.

PTE Academic is an integrated skills test. Some item types in this part of the test also assess writing and reading skills.

Section 1

The first section in the listening part, *Summarize spoken text*, is an integrated skills item type that tests listening and writing skills. Two to three items of this type appear, depending on the combination of items in a given test.

Section 2

In Section 2, there is a single timed listening section consisting of 15–22 items, depending on the combination of items in a given test. You will have approximately 23–28 minutes to complete this section. Different response formats are used in the listening part of PTE Academic.

Since listening takes place in real time, PTE Academic assesses your ability to process spoken language in real time. Each recording is played only once. You can take notes using the Erasable Noteboard Booklet provided when listening to the recording, and use these notes as a guide to complete the tasks.

Scoring

All items in PTE Academic are machine scored. Scores for some item types are based on correctness alone, while others are centered on correctness, formal aspects and the quality of your response.

Formal aspects refer to the form of your response, for example, whether it is over or under the word limit for a particular item type, or whether it contains more than one sentence for an item type requiring a one-sentence response.

The **quality** of your response is represented in a number of additional skills called Enabling Skills. For example, in the item type *Re-tell lecture* your response will be scored on skills such as oral fluency and pronunciation. Scores for item types assessing speaking and writing skills are generated by automated scoring systems. For information about automated scoring, please refer to www.pearsonpte.com.

Types of scoring

There are two types of scoring.

➤ **Correct or incorrect**

Some item types are scored as either **correct** or **incorrect.** If your responses to these items are correct, you will receive the maximum score points available for each item type. If your responses are incorrect, you will receive no score points.

➤ **Partial credit**

Other item types are scored as **correct**, **partially correct** or **incorrect**. If your responses to these items are correct, you will receive the maximum score points available for each item type. If your responses are partially correct, you will receive some score points, but less than the maximum score points available for each item type. If your responses are incorrect, you will receive no score points. This type of scoring is referred to as "partial credit" scoring.

Three item types in the test are scored slightly differently to the others: Multiple-choice, choose multiple answers (Reading), Multiple-choice, choose multiple answers (Listening) and Highlight incorrect words. For these item types, if you get any answers wrong, points will be deducted. For example, if you score two points for two correct answers and then choose two wrong answers, your score will be zero (2–2 = 0). This does not apply to any other item types in the test.

The table below shows the item types that are scored as correct or incorrect, and where partial credit scoring applies.

Part of test	Item type	Skills assessed	Type of scoring
Part 1: Speaking and writing	Personal introduction	Not assessed	Unscored
	Read aloud	Reading and speaking	Partial credit
	Repeat sentence	Listening and speaking	Partial credit
	Describe image	Speaking	Partial credit
	Re-tell lecture	Listening and speaking	Partial credit
	Answer short question	Listening and speaking	Correct/incorrect
	Summarize written text	Reading and writing	Partial credit
	Write essay	Writing	Partial credit
Part 2: Reading	Multiple-choice, choose single answer	Reading	Correct/incorrect
	Multiple-choice, choose multiple answers	Reading	Partial credit*
	Re-order paragraphs	Reading	Partial credit
	Reading: Fill in the blanks	Reading	Partial credit
	Reading & writing: Fill in the blanks	Reading and writing	Partial credit
Part 3: Listening	Summarize spoken text	Listening and writing	Partial credit
	Multiple-choice, choose multiple answers	Listening	Partial credit*
	Fill in the blanks	Listening and writing	Partial credit
	Highlight correct summary	Listening and reading	Correct/incorrect
	Multiple-choice, choose single answer	Listening	Correct/incorrect
	Select missing word	Listening	Correct/incorrect
	Highlight incorrect words	Listening and reading	Partial credit*
	Write from dictation	Listening and writing	Partial credit

*Points deducted for incorrect answers

Types of scores

PTE Academic reports an overall score, communicative skills scores and enabling skills scores.

➤ **Overall score:** The overall score is based on your performance on all test items. For each item, the score you obtain contributes to the overall score. The score range for the overall score is 10–90 points.

➤ **Communicative skills scores:** The communicative skills measured are listening, reading, speaking and writing. The scores for integrated skills items (that is, those assessing reading and speaking, listening and speaking, reading and writing, listening and writing or listening and reading) contribute to the score for each of the communicative skills that the items assess. The score range for each communicative skill is 10–90 points.

➤ **Enabling skills scores:** The enabling skills measured are grammar, oral fluency, pronunciation, spelling, vocabulary and written discourse. The scores for enabling skills are based on your performance on only those items that assess these skills specifically. The score range for each enabling skill is 10–90 points.

- **Grammar:** the correct use of language with respect to word form and word order at the sentence level

- **Oral fluency:** the smooth, effortless and natural-paced delivery of speech

- **Pronunciation:** the production of speech sounds in a way that is easily understandable to most regular speakers of the language. Regional or national varieties of English pronunciation are considered correct to the degree that they are easily understandable to most regular speakers of the language.

- **Spelling:** the writing of words according to the spelling rules of the language. All national variations are considered correct, but one spelling convention should be used consistently in a given response.

- **Vocabulary:** the appropriate choice of words used to express meaning, as well as lexical range

- **Written discourse:** the correct and communicatively efficient production of written language at the textual level. Written discourse skills are represented in the structure of a written text, its internal coherence, logical development and the range of linguistic resources used to express meaning precisely.

The scores for enabling skills are not awarded when your responses are inappropriate for the items in either content or form. For example, if an essay task requires you to discuss global warming and you provide a response entirely devoted to the topic of fashion design, you will not receive any score points for writing or any of the enabling skills assessed by the item. In relation to form, if a task requires a one-sentence summary of a text and you give a list of words, you will not be awarded any score points for your response to that item.

Score report

The image on the next page shows an example PTE Academic score report that you will receive after you have completed the test. The report shows your overall score, communicative skills scores and enabling skills scores.

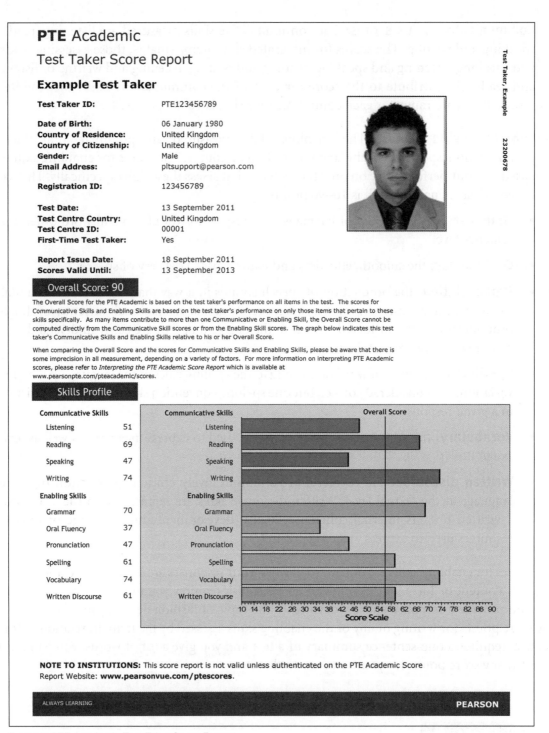

PTE Academic
Test Taker Score Report

Example Test Taker

Test Taker ID:	PTE123456789
Date of Birth:	06 January 1980
Country of Residence:	United Kingdom
Country of Citizenship:	United Kingdom
Gender:	Male
Email Address:	pltsupport@pearson.com
Registration ID:	123456789
Test Date:	13 September 2011
Test Centre Country:	United Kingdom
Test Centre ID:	00001
First-Time Test Taker:	Yes
Report Issue Date:	18 September 2011
Scores Valid Until:	13 September 2013

Test Taker, Example   23200678

Overall Score: 90

The Overall Score for the PTE Academic is based on the test taker's performance on all items in the test. The scores for Communicative Skills and Enabling Skills are based on the test taker's performance on only those items that pertain to these skills specifically. As many items contribute to more than one Communicative or Enabling Skill, the Overall Score cannot be computed directly from the Communicative Skill scores or from the Enabling Skill scores. The graph below indicates this test taker's Communicative Skills and Enabling Skills relative to his or her Overall Score.

When comparing the Overall Score and the scores for Communicative Skills and Enabling Skills, please be aware that there is some imprecision in all measurement, depending on a variety of factors. For more information on interpreting PTE Academic scores, please refer to *Interpreting the PTE Academic Score Report* which is available at www.pearsonpte.com/pteacademic/scores.

Skills Profile

Communicative Skills

Listening	51
Reading	69
Speaking	47
Writing	74

Enabling Skills

Grammar	70
Oral Fluency	37
Pronunciation	47
Spelling	61
Vocabulary	74
Written Discourse	61

NOTE TO INSTITUTIONS: This score report is not valid unless authenticated on the PTE Academic Score Report Website: **www.pearsonvue.com/ptescores**.

ALWAYS LEARNING   **PEARSON**

Example PTE Academic Test Taker Score Report

Score scale

The score scale on the example score report indicates that the minimum number of points awarded in PTE Academic is 10 and the maximum is 90.

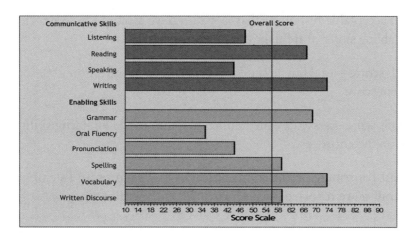

A score of 10 indicates that you have demonstrated English at a level that is not adequate for communication purposes. Scores above 85 indicate an extremely high level of English, and one that is achieved by few language learners.

The score scale shows increments of four score points. For example, the next score after 10 is 14, then 18 and so on.

Item scoring

The diagram below illustrates how different types of scores reported in the PTE Academic score report are computed at the item level.

Integrated speaking item (assessing listening and speaking skills): *Re-tell lecture*

> *You will hear a lecture. After listening to the lecture, in 10 seconds, please speak into the microphone and retell what you have just heard from the lecture in your own words. You will have 40 seconds to give your response.*

Your response is scored on:

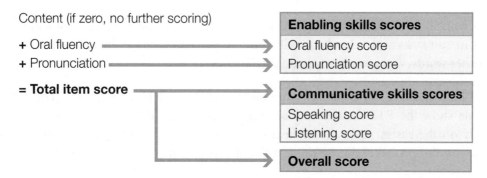

The item is first scored on content. If you give no response or an irrelevant response, the content is scored as 0.

If you provide an acceptable response (that is, you receive a score for content), the item will be scored on two enabling skills: **oral fluency** and **pronunciation**.

The enabling skills scores—oral fluency and pronunciation—in addition to the content score, add up to the **total item score.**

Each enabling skills score assessed by the item contributes to the **enabling skills scores** reported for performance on the entire test.

The total item score contributes to the **communicative skills scores** for listening and speaking, as well as to the **overall score** reported for performance on the entire test.

PTE Academic scores and the Common European Framework

PTE Academic is aligned to the Common European Framework of Reference for Languages (CEF or CEFR), a widely recognized benchmark for language ability. The CEF includes a set of language levels defined by descriptors of language competencies.

The six-level framework was developed by the Council of Europe (2001) to allow language learners, teachers, universities or potential employers to compare and relate language qualifications gained in different educational contexts.

The CEF describes language proficiency in listening, reading, speaking, and writing on a six-level scale, grouped into three bands: A1–A2 (Basic User), B1–B2 (Independent User), C1–C2 (Proficient User).

For further information on the CEF descriptors of language competencies, see Appendix.

The explanation of this alignment is that to have a reasonable chance at successfully performing any of the tasks described at a particular CEF level, you must be able to show that you can do the average tasks at that level.

As you grow in ability, for example, within the B1 level, you will become successful at doing even the most difficult tasks at that level and will also find you can manage the easiest tasks at the next level. In other words, you are entering into the B2 level.

The table below shows PTE Academic scores aligned to the CEF levels A2 to C2. The dotted lines on the scale show the PTE Academic score ranges that predict that you are likely to perform successfully on the easiest tasks at the next higher level. For example, if you score 51 on PTE Academic, you can probably do the more difficult tasks in the CEF B1 level and the easier tasks at B2.

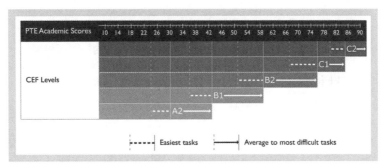

Preliminary alignment of PTE Academic scores to CEF levels

Scores required

A score of **at least 36** is required for the United Kingdom Border Agency (UKBA) Tier 4 visas for students wanting to study on a course below degree level.

A score of **at least 51** is needed for the United Kingdom Border Agency (UKBA) Tier 4 visas for students who want to study on a course at or above degree level at an institution that is not a UK higher education institution.

If you want to study at degree level or above at a UK higher education institution, it is the university that decides on the score you will need. Our experience suggests that most universities in the United Kingdom, United States and Australia require for:

- **undergraduate studies** a minimum score **between 51 and 61**
- **postgraduate studies** a minimum score **between 57 and 67**
- **MBA studies** a minimum score between **59 and 69**

For the latest information on score requirements, visit www.pearsonpte.com.

What PTE Academic scores mean

PTE Academic alignment with the CEF can only be fully understood if it is supported with information showing what it really means to be 'at a level.' In other words, are you likely to be successful with some or all the tasks, even the most difficult ones, at a particular level? The table below shows which PTE Academic scores predict the likelihood of you performing successfully on the easiest, average and most difficult tasks within CEF levels A2 to C2.

PTE Academic scores predicting the likelihood of successful performance on CEF level tasks			
CEF level	Easiest	Average	Most difficult
C2	80	85	NA
C1	67	76	84
B2	51	59	75
B1	36	43	58
A2	24	30	42

For example, if your PTE Academic score is 36, this predicts that you will perform successfully on the easiest tasks at B1. From 36 to 43, the likelihood of successfully performing the easiest tasks develops into doing well on the average tasks at B1. Finally, reaching 58 predicts that you will perform well at the most difficult B1 level tasks.

You can use the table below to find out what PTE Academic scores in the range 10 to 84 (A1 to C1) mean. It shows the score ranges that predict some degree of performance at the next level, and it explains what you are likely to be able to do within those score ranges.

PTE Academic score	Common European Framework level	Level Descriptor © Council of Europe	What does this mean for a score user?
76–84	C1	Can understand a wide range of demanding, longer texts and recognize implicit meaning. Can express him/herself fluently and spontaneously without much obvious searching for expressions. Can use language flexibly and effectively for social, academic and professional purposes. Can produce clear, well-structured, detailed text on complex subjects, showing controlled use of organizational patterns, connectors and cohesive devices.	C1 is a level at which a student can comfortably participate in all post-graduate activities, including teaching. It is not required for students entering university at undergraduate level. Most international students who enter university at a B2 level would acquire a level close to or at C1 after living in the country for several years, and actively participating in all language activities encountered at university.

PTE Academic score	Common European Framework level	Level Descriptor © Council of Europe	What does this mean for a score user?
59–75	B2	Can understand the main ideas of complex text on both concrete and abstract topics, including technical discussions in his/her field of specialization. Can interact with a degree of fluency and spontaneity that makes regular interaction with native speakers quite possible without strain for either party. Can produce clear, detailed text on a wide range of subjects and explain a viewpoint on a topical issue giving the advantages and disadvantages of various options.	B2 was designed as the level required to participate independently in higher level language interaction. It is typically the level required to be able to follow academic instruction and to participate in academic education, including both coursework and student life.
51–58	Predicts success on easiest tasks at B2	Has sufficient command of the language to deal with most familiar situations, but will often require repetition and make many mistakes. Can deal with standard spoken language, but will have problems in noisy circumstances. Can exchange factual information on familiar routine and non-routine matters within his/her field with some confidence. Can pass on a detailed piece of information reliably. Can understand the information content of the majority of recorded or broadcast material on topics of personal interest delivered in clear standard speech.	

PTE Academic score	Common European Framework level	Level Descriptor © Council of Europe	What does this mean for a score user?
43–58	B1	Can understand the main points of clear standard input on familiar matters regularly encountered in work, school, leisure, etc. Can deal with most situations likely to arise whilst in an area where the language is spoken. Can produce simple connected text on topics, which are familiar or of personal interest. Can describe experiences and events, dreams, hopes and ambitions and briefly give reasons and explanations for opinions and plans.	B1 is insufficient for full academic level participation in language activities. A student at this level could 'get by' in everyday situations independently. To be successful at communication in university settings, additional English language courses are required.
36–42	Predicts success on easiest tasks at B1	Has limited command of language, but it is sufficient in most familiar situations provided language is simple and clear. May be able to deal with less routine situations on public transport e.g., asking another passenger where to get off for an unfamiliar destination. Can re-tell short written passages in a simple fashion using the wording and ordering of the original text. Can use simple techniques to start, maintain or end a short conversation. Can tell a story or describe something in a simple list of points.	

PTE Academic score	Common European Framework level	Level Descriptor © Council of Europe	What does this mean for a score user?
30–42	A2	Can understand sentences and frequently used expressions related to areas of most immediate relevance (e.g., very basic personal and family information, shopping, local geography, employment). Can communicate in simple and routine tasks requiring a simple and direct exchange of information on familiar and routine matters. Can describe in simple terms aspects of his/her background, immediate environment and matters in areas of immediate need.	A2 is an insufficient level for academic level participation.
10–29	A1 or below	Can understand and use familiar everyday expressions and very basic phrases aimed at the satisfaction of needs of a concrete type. Can introduce him/herself and others and can ask and answer questions about personal details such as where he/she lives, people he/she knows and things he/she has. Can interact in a simple way provided the other person talks slowly and clearly and is prepared to help.	A1 is an insufficient level for academic level participation.

In Chapters 3–6 of the *Official Guide*, you will practice PTE Academic item types and compare your responses with sample responses rated at the CEF levels C1, B2 and B1. This will allow you to evaluate your current proficiency level and assess any progress you make by studying English.

PTE Academic

Preparation

Test preparation

Test preparation includes familiarizing yourself with the test format, evaluating your proficiency level, making decisions about when to take the test, creating a study plan to improve knowledge and skills in English, and studying test-taking tips.

Test format

If you know exactly what to expect in advance, you will approach the test with greater confidence. The test format includes features such as:

➤ **Length and timing:** How long does each part of PTE Academic last? How much time is allowed for each section and each item type?

➤ **Quantity:** How many parts are included in the test? How many sections are included in each part? How many items are included in one section?

➤ **Layout:** How is each item type presented on screen?

➤ **Instructions:** What task needs to be completed for each item type? How are responses recorded?

➤ **Item types:** How are different item types presented on screen? What tasks need to be completed? What skills are assessed? How are responses scored?

Information about the test format of PTE Academic and item type practice are included in Chapters 3–6. The CD-ROM included with this guide offers a lot of additional practice materials. You can also refer to "Resources" in this chapter for information on other test preparation resources.

Evaluating your English proficiency

Before taking PTE Academic, you should determine whether you are ready to take the test. There are two points to consider:

- the target or minimum test score required for your purposes
- your current English proficiency level

To find out the minimum test score you must achieve, consult the college or institution that you are applying to, as well as your sponsor if relevant.

To find out your current English proficiency level and whether you are ready to take PTE Academic, you can take a PTE Academic practice test at www.pearsonpte.com.

Deciding when to take the test

If you attain your target score in a practice test, or if you believe that your proficiency level matches the score you require, you can register to take PTE Academic at your earliest convenience. However, if there is a considerable gap between your score in a practice test and your target score, you should take the test at a later stage. A summary of the steps to help you decide when to take the test is shown below.

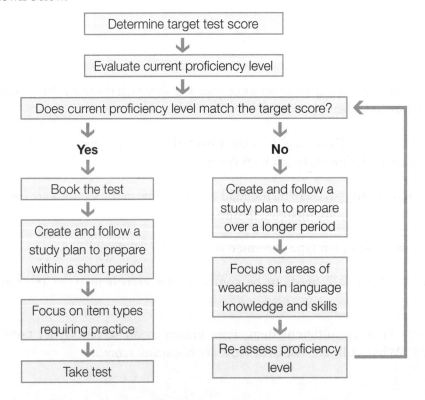

Creating a study plan

When you decide to take the test, you should plan carefully so that you can make the most profitable use of the time available to prepare. In other words, you should create a study plan.

Preparing within a short period

If you decide to take the test within a short period, your preparation should be test-focused rather than general. You should produce a study plan accordingly.

- Use all the test-related resources listed in "Resources" in this chapter.
- Familiarize yourself with the test format using the resources you have obtained.
- Do the item practice in the guide and on the CD-ROM as recommended on page xi and in the CD-ROM Introduction.
- Make a list of the item types which you find difficult.
- Plan to do selective practice, focusing on each of the item types in the list.
- Try to increase your use of test-taking strategies. Strategies for responding to each item type in the test are included in Chapters 3–6.
- Create a study schedule. This could be daily or weekly, depending on how much time you have before the test.
- Make a commitment and follow your study schedule.
- Review your progress regularly and adjust your schedule accordingly.
- Take another practice test to assess your performance, and repeat the steps above until you feel confident in your ability to handle all item types in the test.

Preparing over a longer period

If you decide to take the test at a later stage, you should aim to improve your general and academic English proficiency over a longer period. You can do this by self-study, or by taking a taught English course, or a mixture of the two.

If you choose to do self-study, your study plan may include the following:

- Identify your general strengths and weaknesses in language knowledge and skills.
- Make a list of language knowledge and skills that you want to improve, in order of priority.
- Identify and obtain the learning and practice materials you need.
- Create a study schedule. This could be daily or weekly, depending on how much time you have for study.
- Study and practice, focusing on the language skills that you want to improve.
- Make a commitment and follow your study schedule.
- Review your progress regularly and adjust your schedule accordingly.
- Use general proficiency tests and PTE Academic practice tests to regularly review your progress.
- Follow the steps for "Preparing within a short period" when you determine that your proficiency level matches your target score.

General test-taking tips

In addition to the test-taking strategies included in Chapters 3–6, there are some general pieces of advice which apply to all test situations:

- Get a good night's sleep the night before the test. It is better to go to bed early than to do last-minute studying.
- Make sure you have the correct documentation and ID to take to the test center as listed in the *Test Taker Handbook.*
- Allow yourself plenty of time to reach the test center. There may be unavoidable delays. If you have to rush to get to the test center, you might feel anxious when taking the test.
- Read the test instructions carefully, and follow them exactly.
- Read ahead if possible. For example, while you are waiting for a recording to start, read the questions to get an idea of what you are going to hear.
- Do not spend too much time on a single item.
- Stay focused. Do not worry about other items that you have already responded to or will answer later in the test.
- Spend any available time checking your answers. Remember, you cannot navigate back in the test to check answers later.

Resources

In addition to this guide, there are a number of resources available at www.pearsonpte.com to help you learn about and prepare for PTE Academic.

➤ Test Tutorial

The *PTE Academic Tutorial* (available in Flash and PDF formats) is a free resource that provides you with a detailed overview of the test, guidance on how to navigate through it, and instructions on answering the different item types.

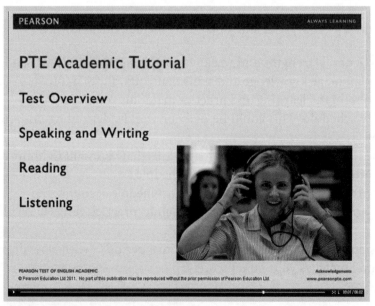

PTE Academic Tutorial

➤ **Test taking strategies**

Test taking strategies is a set of self-study lessons that give you a three-step approach to successfully answering each of the 20 item types in the test.

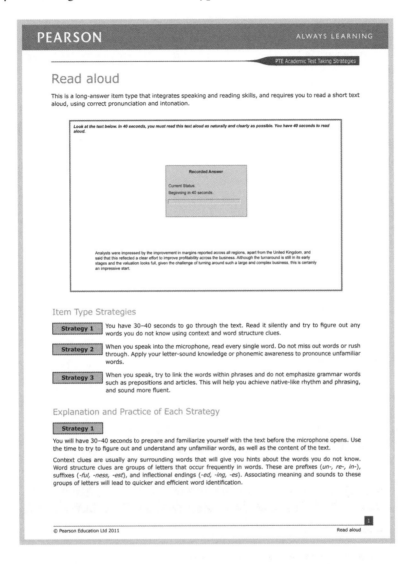

➤ Test preparation courses

If you want some help studying for the test, you can contact one of our professional partners who offer PTE Academic preparation courses.

Prepare for PTE Academic with courses run by our professional partners:

Australia

Bangladesh

China

India

Israel

Pakistan

Singapore

UK

US

Preparation courses

➤ Practice tests

On- and offline practice tests give you the opportunity to practice all your skills, gain full experience of the test format and items, and assess your progress.

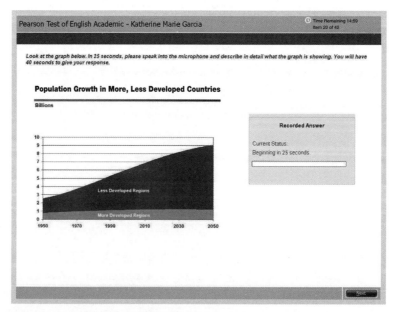

PTE Academic practice tests

➤ **Test Taker Handbook**

The *Test Taker Handbook* gives you all the information you need about registering for and booking a test, payment, ID requirements, and what to expect on the day of your test. It is available in eight different languages.

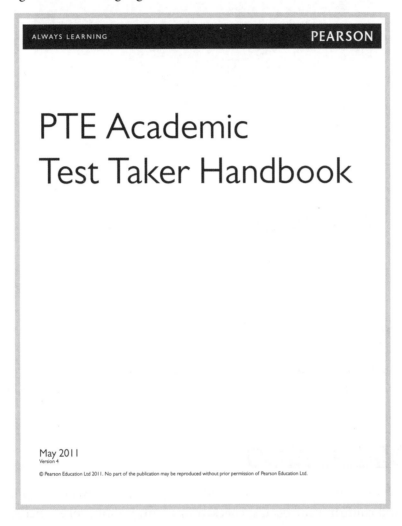

ALWAYS LEARNING   **PEARSON**

PTE Academic Test Taker Handbook

May 2011
Version 4

© Pearson Education Ltd 2011. No part of the publication may be reproduced without prior permission of Pearson Education Ltd.

New resources and information are regularly added to the Pearson website at www.pearsonpte.com.

Registration and scheduling

The first step towards taking PTE Academic is registration. Before you can book a test, you must create a web account by registering your details on the Pearson Tests of English website. This can be done online 24 hours a day, seven days a week, or by calling one of Pearson's customer service teams during working hours. For contact details, refer to the *Test Taker Handbook*, which can be downloaded at www.pearsonpte.com. After you have registered, you will receive a user name and password which can be used to sign in and schedule your test. Start the registration process by visiting the Pearson Tests of English website at www.pearsonpte.com.

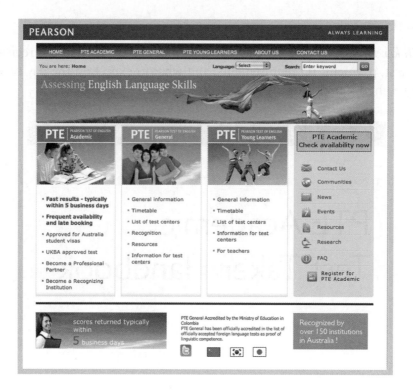

On test day

You need to arrive at the test center at least 30 minutes before your scheduled test time. This will allow enough time to sign in and follow all the necessary procedures at the test center.

Arriving at the test center

Upon arriving at the test center, you will need to sign in at the main reception desk. A Test Administrator will confirm your details, check your identification, collect necessary biometrics and explain the test center rules and regulations.

➤ **ID requirements**

You are required to present one valid, unexpired form of identification before taking the test. Acceptable ID varies by country, and full details can be found in the *Test Taker Handbook*, which can be downloaded at www.pearsonpte.com.

➤ **Biometrics**

Due to the high levels of security at Pearson test centers, test taker biometrics will be collected. Biometrics may include, but are not limited to, photographs, signatures, fingerprints and palm vein scans.

> ## Rules and regulations

Before entering the testing room, you will be asked to read and agree to the PTE Academic Test Taker Rules Agreement. This outlines the procedures and rules you need to follow while taking your test at the test center. Non-disclosure of information is included as part of the agreement, which means that you agree not to publish, reproduce or transmit the test (in whole or in part). You will be reminded about this agreement when you log in to a test delivery workstation and begin the test. Unacceptable behavior or failure to follow any of the rules and regulations may result in you not being allowed into the testing room, or being expelled from the test center. If you are not able to take your test due to a breach of the test taker rules, your test will be marked as a "No Show," and no refund will be given.

You are not allowed to bring any personal belongings (such as mobile phones, pagers, coats, watches, wallets, MP3 players, etc.) into the testing room. The test center will provide secure storage facilities where you can keep your belongings during the test. You may prefer to leave some of these items at home.

The Test Administrator will provide you with an Erasable Noteboard Booklet and pen so that you can take notes during the test. When you enter the testing room, you will not be allowed to take any notes until the test has started.

Taking the test

The testing room will contain several test delivery workstations separated by partitions and monitored by closed circuit television. When it is time to begin your test, the Test Administrator will assign you a workstation.

The photo below shows test takers in a testing room at a Pearson test center.

Timing

The amount of time given for completing PTE Academic is approximately three hours. There is a timer in the upper right-hand corner of the computer screen, which shows the time remaining on a given section of the test.

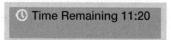

The timer will change to red when there are fewer than five minutes remaining for that section. The timer can be hidden by clicking on the clock icon with the mouse. Click on the icon again to bring it back.

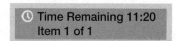

The item counter shows you the number of items in that section.

Pre-test checks

There are a few procedures that you need to go through on screen before starting the test, such as the Non-Disclosure Agreement Reminder and equipment checks.

➤ **Non-Disclosure Agreement Reminder**

After logging in, you will be presented with a Non-Disclosure Agreement (NDA) Reminder. The NDA states that you must not disclose, publish or transmit the test. These terms are presented to you when you book your test, and again when you sign in at the test center. The NDA is repeated to ensure that you understand and agree to the PTE Academic rules before beginning the test.

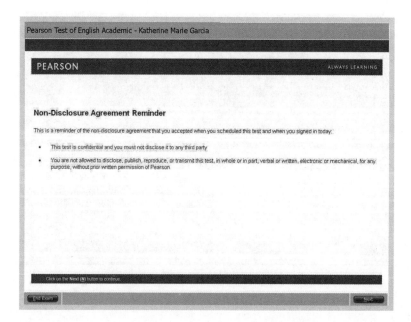

➤ **Welcome and equipment check**

Following the NDA reminder, you will be presented with a welcome screen showing an overview of the test structure and reminding you that the test will take approximately three hours. The image below shows an example of a welcome screen.

You will be given the opportunity to check the equipment before the test begins. The equipment provided includes a headset with a microphone, keyboard and mouse.

First, you will check your headset.

Then you will check your microphone.

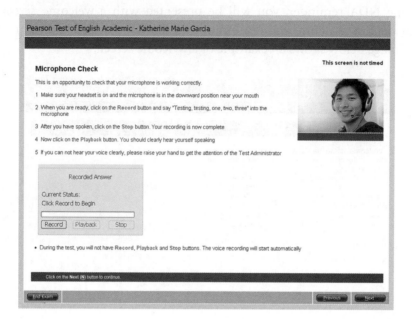

Finally, you should check that you have the correct keyboard for the test. PTE Academic tests should be taken on a QWERTY keyboard. You will check the top row of letters on the keyboard. It is recommended that you practice using a QWERTY keyboard before you take the test.

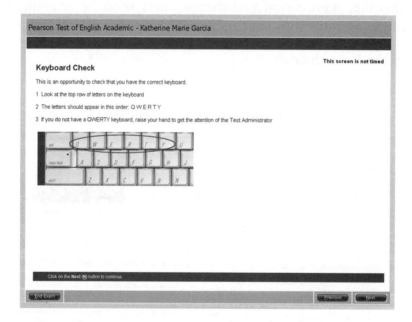

Starting the test

You will see an introduction to key information about PTE Academic. The introduction highlights the four key skills assessed and the three parts of the test. It also mentions the timing, the instructions for each part of the test and the optional break.

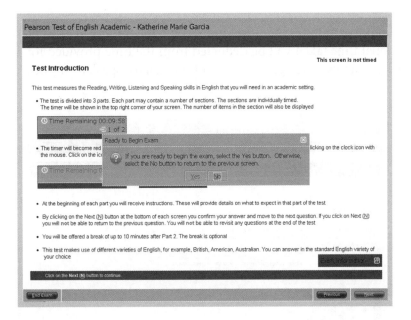

A final reminder warns that the test is about to begin.

During the test

If you click on the "Next" button without giving a response, a warning will appear. Click "No" to return and complete the item. Click "Yes" to skip the item and move to the next screen. You will not be able to return to it later and you will receive zero points for the item.

Items with an audio or video prompt require you to listen to the whole recording. If you click "Next" while the audio or video is playing, you will see a warning message. Click "OK" to return to the item. The audio will continue to play while the message/warning is displayed.

Some very important things to remember whilst doing the test are:

- Use correct punctuation for writing tasks: full stops, capital letters, commas, etc.
- Answer the question. If the question asks you to write or speak about sport, write or speak about sport NOT science.
- Keep strictly within the word limit given for writing tasks.
- Respond quickly and keep speaking during speaking tasks. The microphone will close after three seconds of silence and stop recording.

However, don't:

- write ENTIRELY in capital letters. Only use capitals when needed; at the beginning of sentences, names, etc.
- click "Next" before you have completed the task and are ready to move on.

Taking a break

During the test there is one optional break, which can be taken after you have completed Part 2 of the test. If you decide to take the break, you must leave the testing room for the duration of the break.

Allow yourself about five minutes to return and resume the test before the end of the 10-minute break. Any additional time taken will be deducted from the time provided for Part 3 of the test. You are not allowed to access study guides, make phone calls or speak to any other test takers while taking the break.

Problems during the test

If you experience any problems during the test, remain in your seat and raise your hand for assistance. The Test Administrator will come to you. The Test Administrator cannot answer any questions relating to the content of the test.

Finishing the test

At the end of the test you will be asked to click on the "End Exam" button on screen and raise your hand to inform the Test Administrator that you have completed the test.

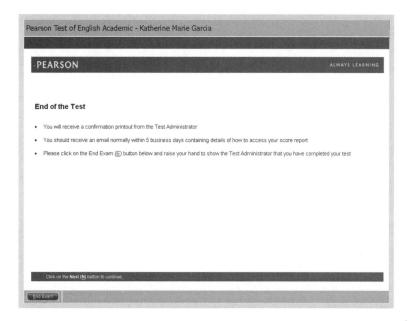

Once you have completed the test, leave the testing room and return to the main reception desk. The Test Administrator will provide you with an End of Test Confirmation printout. This is not a score report or certificate, but a confirmation that you have completed PTE Academic with information on how and when you will receive your score report.

Before leaving the test center, make sure that you have your End of Test Confirmation printout and have collected all your personal belongings from the storage facilities.

PTE Academic

Speaking

Section 2 of the speaking and writing part of PTE Academic (Part 1) tests your ability to produce spoken English in an academic environment.

Part 1: Speaking and writing		
Section	**Item type**	**Time allowed**
Section 1	Personal introduction	1 minute
Section 2	Read aloud	30–35 minutes
	Repeat sentence	
	Describe image	
	Re-tell lecture	
	Answer short question	
Sections 3–4	Summarize written text	20 minutes
Section 5	Summarize written text or Write essay	10 or 20 minutes
Section 6	Write essay	20 minutes

Speaking skills

The speaking skills tested in PTE Academic include the following:

- speaking for a purpose (to repeat, to inform, to explain)
- reading a text aloud
- supporting an opinion with details, examples and explanations
- organizing an oral presentation in a logical way
- developing complex ideas within a spoken discourse
- using words and phrases appropriate to the context
- using correct grammar
- speaking at a natural rate
- producing fluent speech
- using correct intonation
- using correct pronunciation
- using correct stress
- speaking under timed conditions

Overview

General speaking instructions are presented before Section 2 (speaking).

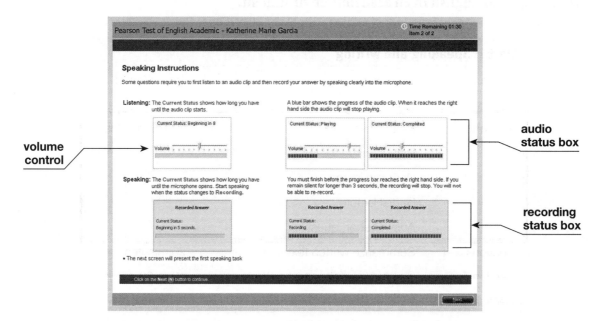

There are one or two status boxes on screen, depending on whether the item type involves listening. The audio status box shows how long until the audio or video recording starts and the progress of the recording while you are listening and/or watching. You can adjust the volume of the recording by moving the slider on the volume control. The recording status box lets you know when to start recording and when to complete your response. You are not able to re-record your response. In addition, if you remain silent for more than three seconds, the microphone will close automatically.

Speaking item types require you to respond orally using fluent speech, correct intonation, stress and pronunciation that are easily understandable to most regular speakers of the language. PTE Academic recognizes regional and national varieties of English pronunciation to the degree that they are understandable to most regular speakers of the language.

Five item types appear in the speaking section of PTE Academic. The total time to complete the speaking section of the test is approximately 30–35 minutes, depending on the combination of items in a given test. Some of the item types are integrated and assess both speaking as well as listening and reading skills.

Section 2 (speaking) total time: 30–35 minutes

Item type	Task	Skills assessed	Text/ Recording length	Time to answer
Read aloud	A text appears on screen. Read the text aloud.	reading and speaking	text up to 60 words	varies by item, depending on the length of text
Repeat sentence	After listening to a sentence, repeat the sentence.	listening and speaking	3–9 seconds	15 seconds
Describe image	An image appears on screen. Describe the image in detail.	speaking	N/A	40 seconds
Re-tell lecture	After listening to or watching a lecture, retell the lecture in your own words.	listening and speaking	up to 90 seconds	40 seconds
Answer short question	After listening to a question, answer with a single word or a few words.	listening and speaking	3–9 seconds	10 seconds

The recordings for the item type *Re-tell lecture* focus on academic subjects in the humanities, natural sciences or social sciences. They contain characteristics of actual speech, such as accents and dialects, fillers, hesitations, false starts, self corrections and variations in delivery speed. Although you may not be familiar with the topics presented, all the information you need to answer the items is contained in the recordings.

Each recording is played only once. You may take notes using the Erasable Noteboard Booklet and pen, and use these notes as a guide when answering the items.

Speaking item types are not timed individually. You can refer to the timer in the upper right-hand corner of the computer screen, "Time Remaining," which counts down the time remaining for the speaking section.

Read aloud

Task

Read aloud is a long-answer speaking item type. It tests your ability to read a short text aloud using correct pronunciation and intonation. It assesses both speaking and reading skills. The image below shows the item type.

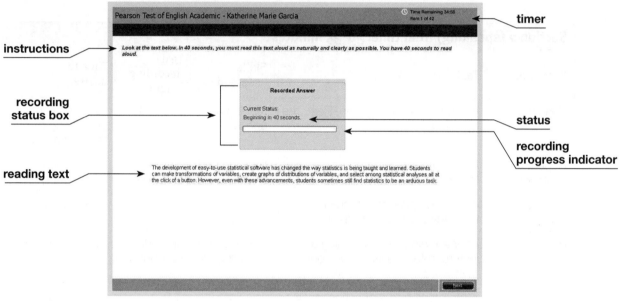

PTE Academic: Read aloud

Below are the features of *Read aloud*.

1 Instructions are presented at the top of the computer screen.

> *Look at the text below. In 40 seconds, you must read this text aloud as naturally and clearly as possible. You have 40 seconds to read aloud.*

2 In the recording status box, the status will count down from 40 seconds.

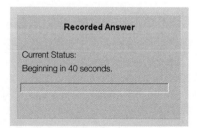

The amount of time you have to prepare will vary by item. The time will be stated in the instructions. In the case of the current example, you have 40 seconds to prepare.

3 A reading text follows.

> The development of easy-to-use statistical software has changed the way statistics is being taught and learned. Students can make transformations of variables, create graphs of distributions of variables, and select among statistical analyses all at the click of a button. However, even with these advancements, students sometimes still find statistics to be an arduous task.

4 After 40 seconds, you will hear a short tone and the microphone will open. In the recording status box, the status will change to "Recording."

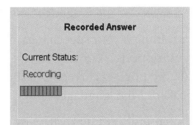

The recording progress indicator represents the entire duration the microphone is open. So if the text is short, the bar moves faster. If the text is long, the bar moves slower.

The recording progress indicator features a blue bar that will gradually move to the right. If you stop speaking for more than three seconds, or if time runs out, the status will change to "Completed." The amount of time you have to respond will vary by item. The time will be stated in the instructions. In the case of the current example, you have 40 seconds to give your response.

You should not read punctuation marks aloud. For example, if a phrase is set off by quotation marks, do not say, "quotation mark." Only read aloud the words in the text. A comma may require a short pause. Read the text naturally.

5 Click on the "Next" button to go to the next item. The timer for the speaking section will continue running.

The reading texts for this item type are up to 60 words in length. There are six to seven *Read aloud* items in PTE Academic, depending on the combination of items in a given test. They are presented together in a single block. The amount of time you have to respond to each item will vary. The time will be stated in the instructions.

Scoring

Your score on *Read aloud* is based on three factors:

➤ **Content:** Does your response include all the words in the reading text, and only these words?

Content is scored by counting the number of correct words in your response. Replacements. insertions and omissions of words will negatively affect your score.

➤ **Oral fluency:** Does your response demonstrate a smooth, effortless and natural rate of speech?

Oral fluency is scored by determining if your rhythm, phrasing and stress are smooth. The best responses are spoken at a constant and natural rate of speech with appropriate phrasing. Hesitations, repetitions and false starts will negatively affect your score.

➤ **Pronunciation:** Does your response demonstrate your ability to produce speech sounds in a similar way to most regular speakers of the language?

Pronunciation is scored by determining if your speech is easily understandable to most regular speakers of the language. The best responses contain vowels and consonants pronounced in a native-like way, and stress words and phrases correctly. Responses should also be immediately understandable to a regular speaker of the language.

PTE Academic recognizes regional and national varieties of English pronunciation to the degree that they are understandable to most regular speakers of the language.

Partial credit scoring applies to *Read aloud*. No credit is given for no response or an irrelevant response. This item type affects the scoring of the following:

Overall score			✔
Communicative skills			
Listening		Speaking	✔
Reading	✔	Writing	
Enabling skills			
Grammar		Spelling	
Oral fluency	✔	Vocabulary	
Pronunciation	✔	Written discourse	

Speaking and reading skills

Read aloud is an integrated skills item type that tests both your speaking and reading skills in an academic environment. Below are the key skills tested:

Speaking

- speaking for a purpose (to repeat, to inform, to explain)
- reading a text aloud
- speaking at a natural rate
- producing fluent speech
- using correct intonation
- using correct pronunciation
- using correct stress
- speaking under timed conditions

Reading

- identifying a writer's purpose, style, tone, or attitude
- understanding academic vocabulary
- reading a text under timed conditions

Your listening and writing skills are not tested by this item type.

Strategies

Before speaking

- Read the text before the microphone opens. You have between 30 and 40 seconds to do this.
- Focus on the content of the text. Some features of speech, such as phrasing and intonation, convey overall meaning. You can only deliver them correctly if you understand what you are reading.
- Briefly rehearse any unknown words, following normal spelling and pronunciation conventions.
- Speak when you hear the tone. Sit up straight and take a deep breath—this will help you speak clearly.

While speaking

- Imagine that you are reading to an audience that is interested in what you are saying. Speak in such a way that you help the imaginary audience to understand.

  — Speak clearly and at a normal speed. Avoid speaking too quickly as there is plenty of time.
  — Speak at a normal volume. If you speak too softly, it may be difficult to score your response.
  — Use the punctuation, such as commas, semi-colons and periods, as a guide for pauses and sentence stress.

- Make an attempt at unknown words and then move on.
- Do not go back to correct yourself or hesitate. If you make a mistake, continue reading. The microphone will close after three seconds of silence.

- Give a single response demonstrating your best ability. You will not be able to re-record your response.
- Go on to the next item if you finish speaking before the recording progress indicator reaches the end.

Practice

Below is a *Read aloud* item for you to respond to.

⏱ **35 sec.** **Read the text aloud as naturally and clearly as possible. To simulate the test conditions, give yourself only 35 seconds to respond to this item.**

> Photography's gaze widened during the early years of the twentieth century and, as the snapshot camera became increasingly popular, the making of photographs became increasingly available to a wide cross-section of the public. The British people grew accustomed to, and were hungry for, the photographic image.

Record your response and compare it with the sample responses on the Audio CD.

Remember, during PTE Academic you will give your response by speaking into a microphone at a test delivery workstation.

Answer key p.174 **Now check the Answer key.**

Repeat sentence

Task

Repeat sentence is a short-answer speaking item type. It tests your ability to understand and remember a sentence, and then repeat the sentence exactly as you hear it using correct pronunciation. It assesses both speaking and listening skills. The image below shows the item type.

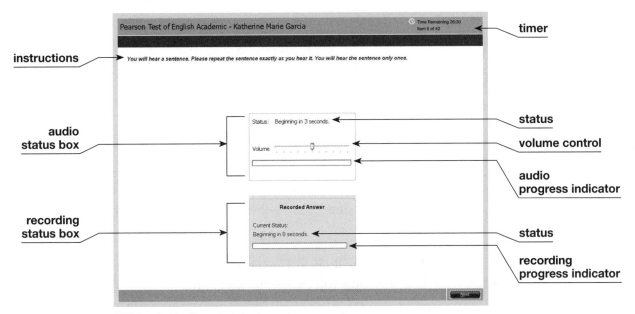

PTE Academic: Repeat sentence

Below are the features of *Repeat sentence*.

1 Instructions are presented at the top of the computer screen.

> *You will hear a sentence. Please repeat the sentence exactly as you hear it. You will hear the sentence only once.*

2 There are two status boxes for *Repeat sentence*. The first is the audio status box. In the audio status box, the status will count down from three seconds. Then a recording will play automatically.

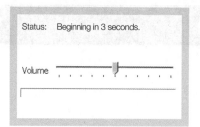

The audio progress indicator represents the entire duration of the recording. So if the recording is short, the bar moves faster. If the recording is long, the bar moves slower.

The status will change to "Playing." To adjust the volume of the recording, move the slider left to decrease and right to increase. You can adjust the volume at any time while the recording is playing. The audio progress indicator features a blue bar that will gradually move to the right as the recording continues. When the recording finishes, the status will change to "Completed."

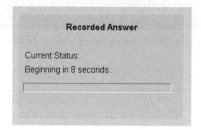

In the recording status box, the status will start counting down at the same time as the audio status box. The status will count down while the recording is playing. When the recording finishes, the status will count down one second—the time you have before you respond.

3 After one second, the microphone will open. There is no tone before the microphone opens. In the recording status box, the status will change to "Recording."

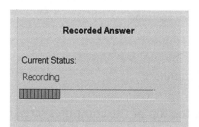

The recording progress indicator represents the entire duration the microphone is open. So if the sentence is short, the bar moves faster. If the sentence is long, the bar moves slower.

The recording progress indicator features a blue bar that will gradually move to the right. If you stop speaking for more than three seconds, or if time runs out, the status will change to "Completed." You have 15 seconds to give your response.

 Play the CD to listen to the recording that goes with this item.

4 Click on the "Next" button to go to the next item. The timer for the speaking section will continue running.

The recordings for this item type run for approximately three to nine seconds. Each recording will play only once. There are 10 to 12 *Repeat sentence* items in PTE Academic, depending on the combination of items in a given test. They are presented together in a single block. You have 15 seconds to record your response to each of these items.

Scoring

Your score on *Repeat sentence* is based on three factors:

➤ **Content:** Does your response include all the words in the sentence, and only these words?

Content is scored by counting the number of correct word sequences in your response. Having almost nothing from the prompt in your response will negatively affect your score.

➤ **Oral fluency:** Does your response demonstrate a smooth, effortless and natural rate of speech?

Oral fluency is scored by determining if your rhythm, phrasing and stress are smooth. The best responses are spoken at a constant and natural rate of speech with appropriate phrasing. Hesitations, repetitions and false starts will negatively affect your score.

➤ **Pronunciation:** Does your response demonstrate your ability to produce speech sounds in a similar way to most regular speakers of the language?

Pronunciation is scored by determining if your speech is easily understandable to most regular speakers of the language. The best responses contain vowels and consonants pronounced in a native-like way, as well as words and phrases stressed correctly. Responses should also be immediately understandable to a regular speaker of the language.

PTE Academic recognizes regional and national varieties of English pronunciation to the degree that they are understandable to most regular speakers of the language.

Partial credit scoring applies to *Repeat sentence*. No credit is given for no response or an irrelevant response. This item type affects the scoring of the following:

Overall score			✔
Communicative skills			
Listening	✔	Speaking	✔
Reading		Writing	
Enabling skills			
Grammar		Spelling	
Oral fluency	✔	Vocabulary	
Pronunciation	✔	Written discourse	

3

Speaking

Listening and speaking skills

Repeat sentence is an integrated skills item type that tests both your listening and speaking skills in an academic environment. Below are the key skills tested:

Listening

- understanding academic vocabulary
- inferring the meaning of unfamiliar words
- comprehending variations in tone, speed, accent

Speaking

- speaking for a purpose (to repeat, to inform, to explain)
- speaking at a natural rate
- producing fluent speech
- using correct intonation
- using correct pronunciation
- using correct stress
- speaking under timed conditions

Your writing skills are not tested by this item type, and your reading skills are only used to read the instructions.

Strategies

While listening

- Try to remember the sentence or take notes. If you want to take notes, write key words and phrases. There will not be time to take complete notes.
- Focus on the meaning of the sentence. This will help you remember the sentence better, and help you use the most appropriate stress and intonation.
- Speak when the status changes to "Recording." There is no tone before the microphone opens on this item type. Sit up straight and take a deep breath—this will help you speak clearly.

While speaking

- Speak clearly and naturally.

  — Do not try to copy the speaker's accent. Speak naturally.
  — Speak at a normal speed. Avoid speaking too quickly as there is plenty of time.
  — Speak at a normal volume. If you speak too softly, it may be difficult to score your response.

- Make an attempt at unknown words and then move on.
- Do not go back to correct yourself or hesitate. If you make a mistake, continue speaking. The microphone will close after three seconds of silence.
- Give a single response demonstrating your best ability. You will not be able to re-record your response.

Practice

Below is a *Repeat sentence* item for you to respond to.

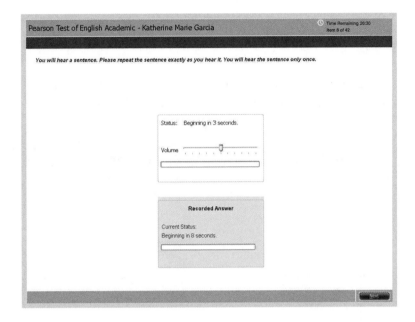

 Listen to the recording only once. Then repeat the sentence exactly as you hear it. To simulate the test conditions, give yourself only 15 seconds to respond to this item.

> Record your response and compare it with the sample responses on the Audio CD.

> Remember, during PTE Academic you will give your response by speaking into a microphone at a test delivery workstation.

Answer key p.174 **Now check the Answer key.**

Describe image

Task

Describe image is a long-answer speaking item type. It tests your ability to describe an image from an academic source. It assesses speaking skills. The screen below shows the item type.

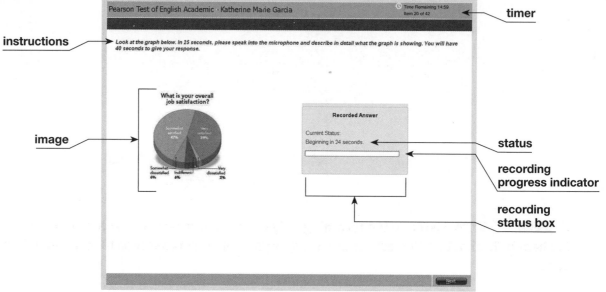

PTE Academic: Describe image

Below are the features of *Describe image*.

1 Instructions are presented at the top of the computer screen.

> *Look at the graph below. In 25 seconds, please speak into the microphone and describe in detail what the graph is showing. You will have 40 seconds to give your response.*

2 An image follows.

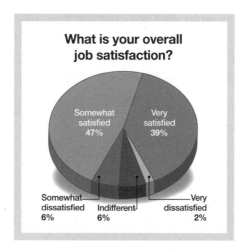

The type of image will vary by item. The image may be a graph, picture, map, chart or table. The type of image will be stated in the instructions. In the case of the current example, the image is a graph.

3 In the recording status box, the status will count down from 25 seconds.

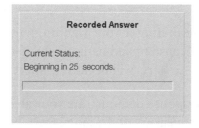

4 After 25 seconds, you will hear a short tone and the microphone will open. The status will change to "Recording."

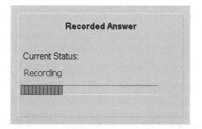

> The recording progress indicator represents the entire duration the microphone is open.

The recording progress indicator features a blue bar that will gradually move to the right. If you stop speaking for more than three seconds, or if time runs out, the status will change to "Completed." You have 40 seconds to give your response.

5 Click on the "Next" button to go to the next item. The timer for the speaking section will continue running.

The images for this item type are authentic images related to academic subjects in the humanities, natural sciences or social sciences. There are six to seven *Describe image* items in PTE Academic, depending on the combination of items in a given test. They are presented together in a single block. You have 40 seconds to record your response to each item.

Scoring

Your score on *Describe image* is based on three factors:

➤ **Content:** Does your response accurately and thoroughly describe the image?

Content is scored by determining if all aspects and elements of the image have been addressed in your response. Your description of relationships, possible developments and conclusions or implications based on details from the image is also scored. The best responses deal with all parts of the image, contain logical and specific information and include possible developments, conclusions or implications. Mentioning just a few disjointed ideas will negatively affect your score.

➤ **Oral fluency:** Does your response demonstrate a smooth, effortless and natural rate of speech?

Oral fluency is scored by determining if your rhythm, phrasing and stress are smooth. The best responses are spoken at a constant and natural rate of speech with appropriate phrasing. Hesitations, repetitions and false starts will negatively affect your score.

➤ **Pronunciation:** Does your response demonstrate your ability to produce speech sounds in a similar way to most regular speakers of the language?

Pronunciation is scored by determining if your speech is easily understandable to most regular speakers of the language. The best responses contain vowels and consonants pronounced in a native-like way, and stress words and phrases correctly. Responses should also be immediately understandable to a regular speaker of the language.

PTE Academic recognizes regional and national varieties of English pronunciation to the degree that they are understandable to most regular speakers of the language.

Partial credit scoring applies to *Describe image*. No credit is given for no response or an irrelevant response. This item type affects the scoring of the following:

Overall score			✔
Communicative skills			
Listening		Speaking	✔
Reading		Writing	
Enabling skills			
Grammar		Spelling	
Oral fluency	✔	Vocabulary	
Pronunciation	✔	Written discourse	

Speaking skills

Describe image tests your speaking skills in an academic environment. Below are the key skills tested:

- speaking for a purpose (to repeat, to inform, to explain)
- supporting an opinion with details, examples and explanations
- organizing an oral presentation in a logical way
- developing complex ideas within a spoken discourse
- using words and phrases appropriate to the context
- using correct grammar
- speaking at a natural rate
- producing fluent speech
- using correct intonation
- using correct pronunciation
- using correct stress
- speaking under timed conditions

Your listening and writing skills are not tested by this item type, and your reading skills are only used to read the instructions.

Strategies

Before speaking

- Study the image. You have 25 seconds to do this. If necessary, take brief notes.

  — First familiarize yourself with the general topic and the type of information conveyed by the image. Check the title, the axes (graphs and charts), the headings and sub-headings (tables) or the labels (maps and pictures).
  — Make sure that you know the units of measurement (US$, kilograms, etc) and the reference points (years, entities, etc) being used.
  — Determine the significant information conveyed by the image. For example, graphs, charts and tables often highlight trends. Maps and pictures usually highlight important features.

- Speak when you hear the tone. Sit up straight and take a deep breath—this will help you speak clearly.

While speaking

- Speak clearly and naturally.

  — Speak at a normal speed. Avoid speaking too quickly as there is plenty of time.
  — Speak at a normal volume. If you speak too softly, it may be difficult to score your response.

- Describe the general content of the image, then summarize the most significant points, referring to details for support.

  — Include all the main points conveyed by the image.
  — Try not to repeat information.

3 Speaking

— When describing developments, conclusions or implications, support your response with details from the image.

- Do not go back to correct yourself or hesitate. If you make a mistake, continue speaking. The microphone will close after three seconds of silence.

Practice

Below is a *Describe image* item for you to respond to.

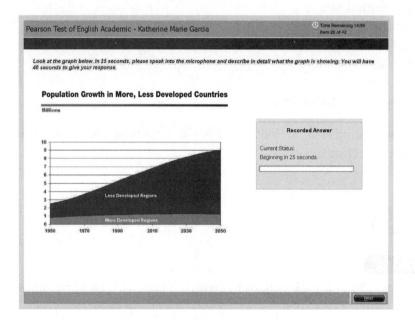

40 sec. **Look at the graph below. Describe in detail what the graph is showing. To simulate the test conditions, give yourself only 40 seconds to respond to this item.**

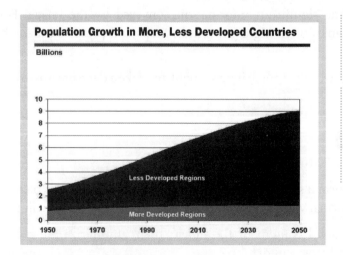

Record your response and compare it with the sample responses on the Audio CD.

Remember, during PTE Academic you will give your response by speaking into a microphone at a test delivery workstation.

Answer key   p.175   **Now check the Answer key.**

Re-tell lecture

Task

Re-tell lecture is a long-answer speaking item type. It tests your ability to give a presentation on information from a lecture on an academic subject. It assesses both speaking and listening skills. The lecture may also be accompanied by an image. The screen below shows the item type.

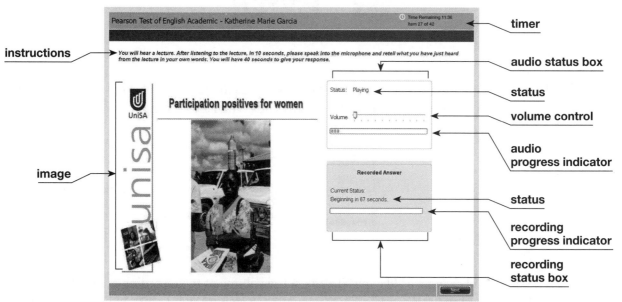

PTE Academic: Re-tell lecture

Below are the features of *Re-tell lecture*.

1 Instructions are presented at the top of the computer screen.

> *You will hear a lecture. After listening to the lecture, in 10 seconds, please speak into the microphone and retell what you have just heard from the lecture in your own words. You will have 40 seconds to give your response.*

2 An image may follow.

3 There are two status boxes for *Re-tell lecture.* The first is the audio status box. In the audio status box, the status will count down from three seconds. Then a recording will play automatically.

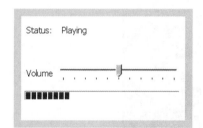

The audio progress indicator represents the entire duration of the recording. So if the recording is short, the bar moves faster. If the recording is long, the bar moves slower.

The status will change to "Playing." To adjust the volume of the recording, move the slider left to decrease and right to increase. You can adjust the volume at any time while the recording is playing. The audio progress indicator features a blue bar that will gradually move to the right as the recording continues. When the recording finishes, the status will change to "Completed."

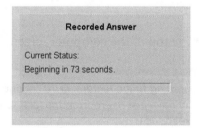

In the recording status box, the status will start counting down at the same time as the audio status box. The status will count down while the recording is playing. When the recording finishes, the status will count down 10 seconds—the time you have before you respond.

4 After 10 seconds, you will hear a short tone and the microphone will open. In the recording status box, the status will change to "Recording."

The recording progress indicator represents the entire duration the microphone is open.

The recording progress indicator features a blue bar that will gradually move to the right. If you stop speaking for more than three seconds, or if time runs out, the status will change to "Completed." You have 40 seconds to give your response.

 Play the CD to listen to the recording that goes with this item.

5 Click on the "Next" button to go to the next item. The timer for the speaking section will continue running.

The recordings for this item type run for approximately 60–90 seconds. Each recording will play only once. There are three to four *Re-tell lecture* items in PTE Academic, depending on the combination of items in a given test. They are presented together in a single block. You have 40 seconds to record your response to each of these items.

Scoring

Your score on *Re-tell lecture* is based on three factors:

➤ **Content:** Does your response accurately and thoroughly retell the information in the lecture?

Content is scored by determining how accurately and thoroughly you convey the situation, characters, aspects, actions and developments presented in the lecture. Your description of relationships, possible developments and conclusions or implications is also scored. The best responses retell all the main points of the lecture and include possible developments, conclusions or implications. Mentioning a few disjointed ideas will negatively affect your score.

➤ **Oral fluency:** Does your response demonstrate a smooth, effortless and natural rate of speech?

Oral fluency is scored by determining if your rhythm, phrasing and stress are smooth. The best responses are spoken at a constant and natural rate of speech with appropriate phrasing. Hesitations, repetitions and false starts will negatively affect your score.

➤ **Pronunciation:** Does your response demonstrate your ability to produce speech sounds in a similar way to most regular speakers of the language?

Pronunciation is scored by determining if your speech is easily understandable to most regular speakers of the language. The best responses contain vowels and consonants pronounced in a native-like way, and stress words and phrases correctly. Responses should also be immediately understandable to a regular speaker of the language.

PTE Academic recognizes regional and national varieties of English pronunciation to the degree that they are understandable to most regular speakers of the language.

Partial credit scoring applies to *Re-tell lecture*. No credit is given for no response or an irrelevant response. This item type affects the scoring of the following:

Overall score			✔
Communicative skills			
Listening	✔	Speaking	✔
Reading		Writing	
Enabling skills			
Grammar		Spelling	
Oral fluency	✔	Vocabulary	
Pronunciation	✔	Written discourse	

Listening and speaking skills

Re-tell lecture is an integrated skills item type that tests both your listening and speaking skills in an academic environment. Below are the key skills tested:

Listening

- identifying the topic, theme or main ideas
- identifying supporting points or examples
- identifying a speaker's purpose, style, tone, or attitude
- understanding academic vocabulary
- inferring the meaning of unfamiliar words
- comprehending explicit and implicit information
- comprehending concrete and abstract information
- classifying and categorizing information
- following an oral sequencing of information
- comprehending variations in tone, speed, accent

Speaking

- speaking for a purpose (to repeat, to inform, to explain)
- supporting an opinion with details, examples and explanations
- organizing an oral presentation in a logical way
- developing complex ideas within a spoken discourse
- using words and phrases appropriate to the context
- using correct grammar

- speaking at a natural rate
- producing fluent speech
- using correct intonation
- using correct pronunciation
- using correct stress
- speaking under timed conditions

Your writing skills are not tested by this item type, and your reading skills are only used to read the instructions.

Strategies

Before listening

- Scan the image, if one is included, quickly. The image will provide the general context for the lecture. You have only three seconds before the recording starts to play automatically.

While listening

- Pay attention to the content of the lecture. It is important that you understand what you hear, because you will have to retell the lecture including all key elements.
- Take notes using the Erasable Noteboard Booklet and pen. Focus on key words. Do not attempt to take notes word-for-word. You may miss important information if you try to write too much.
- Review your notes when the recording stops, and decide how to organize the information. You have 10 seconds to do this.
- Speak when you hear the tone. Sit up straight and take a deep breath—this will help you speak clearly.

While speaking

- Speak clearly and naturally.

    — Speak at a normal speed. Avoid speaking too quickly as there is plenty of time.
    — Speak at a normal volume. If you speak too softly, it may be difficult to score your response.

- Retell the lecture using your notes as a guide. You will have 40 seconds to give your response.

    — Include all of the key points presented in the lecture.
    — Try not to repeat information.

- Do not go back to correct yourself or hesitate. If you make a mistake, continue speaking. The microphone will close after three seconds of silence.

Practice

Below is a *Re-tell lecture* item for you to respond to.

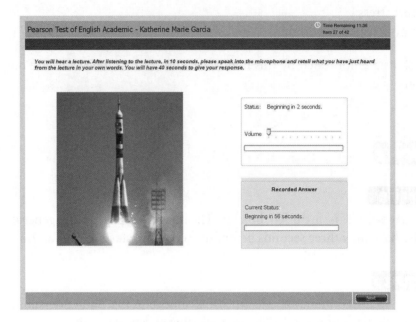

5   40 sec. **Listen to the lecture only once. Then retell what you have just heard from the lecture in your own words. To simulate the test conditions, give yourself only 40 seconds to respond to this item.**

Record your response and compare it with the sample responses on the Audio CD.

Remember, during PTE Academic you will give your response by speaking into a microphone at a test delivery workstation.

Answer key   p.176   **Now check the Answer key.**

Answer short question

Task

Answer short question is a short-answer speaking item type with a single correct response. It tests your ability to understand a question presented in a recording, and provide a brief and accurate response. It assesses both speaking and listening skills. The question may also be accompanied by an image. The screen below shows the item type.

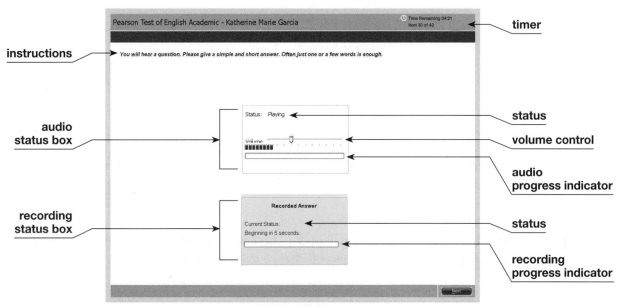

PTE Academic: Answer short question

Below are the features of *Answer short question*.

1 Instructions are presented at the top of the computer screen.

> *You will hear a question. Please give a simple and short answer. Often just one or a few words is enough.*

2 An image may follow.

3 There are two status boxes for *Answer short question*. The first is the audio status box. In the audio status box, the status will count down from three seconds. Then a recording will play automatically.

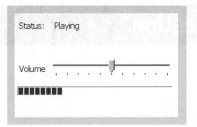

The audio progress indicator represents the entire duration of the recording. So if the recording is short, the bar moves faster. If the recording is long, the bar moves slower.

The status will change to "Playing." To adjust the volume of the recording, move the slider left to decrease and right to increase. You can adjust the volume at any time while the recording is playing. The audio progress indicator features a blue bar that will gradually move to the right as the recording continues. When the recording finishes, the status will change to "Completed."

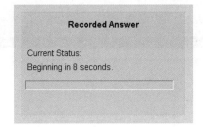

In the recording status box, the status will start counting down at the same time as the audio status box. The status will count down while the recording is playing. When the recording finishes, the status will count down one second—the time you have before you respond.

4 After one second, the microphone will open. There is no tone before the microphone opens. In the recording status box, the status will change to "Recording."

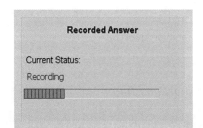

The recording progress indicator represents the entire duration the microphone is open.

The recording progress indicator features a blue bar that will gradually move to the right. If you stop speaking for more than three seconds, or if time runs out, the status will change to "Completed." You have 10 seconds to give your response.

 **Play the CD to listen to the recording that goes with this item.**

5 Click on the "Next" button to go to the next item. The timer for the speaking section will continue running.

The recordings for this item type run for approximately three to nine seconds. Each question will play only once. There are 10 to 12 *Answer short question* items in PTE Academic, depending on the combination of items in a given test. They are presented together in a single block. You have 10 seconds to record your response to each of these items.

Scoring

Your response is scored as either correct or incorrect based on the appropriacy of the words in your response. No credit is given for no response or an incorrect response. This item type affects the scoring of the following:

Overall score			✔
Communicative skills			
Listening	✔	Speaking	✔
Reading		Writing	
Enabling skills			
Grammar		Spelling	
Oral fluency		Vocabulary	✔
Pronunciation		Written discourse	

Listening and speaking skills

Answer short question is an integrated skills item type that tests both your listening and speaking skills in an academic environment. Below are the key skills tested:

Listening

- identifying the topic, theme or main ideas
- understanding academic vocabulary
- inferring the meaning of unfamiliar words

Speaking

- speaking for a purpose (to repeat, to inform, to explain)
- using words and phrases appropriate to the context
- speaking under timed conditions

Your writing skills are not tested by this item type, and your reading skills are only used to read the instructions.

Strategies

While listening

- Listen carefully to the question and determine the type of information your answer requires.
- Speak when the status changes to "Recording." There is no tone on this item type. Sit up straight and take a deep breath—this will help you speak clearly.

While speaking

- Speak clearly and naturally.

  — Speak at a normal speed. Avoid speaking too quickly as there is plenty of time.
  — Speak at a normal volume. If you speak too softly, it may be difficult to score your response.

- Respond with a single word or a short phrase. Do not say more than necessary. You will not get credit for extra words.

Practice

Below is an *Answer short question* item for you to respond to.

7 | 10 sec. **Listen to the recording only once. Then answer the question with one or a few words. To simulate the test conditions, give yourself only 10 seconds to respond to this item.**

Remember, during PTE Academic you will give your response by speaking into a microphone at a test delivery workstation.

Answer key p.177 **Now check the Answer key.**

Improving general speaking skills

Effective speaking

Effective speaking, in both everyday and test situations, requires attention to the five areas listed below. Although not all of these areas will be tested in PTE Academic, improving your skills in each area will help your general language proficiency and improve your overall performance in the test.

➤ **Organization**
- State the purpose clearly. For example, at the beginning of a presentation, explain what the main aims of the presentation are. "Today, I will talk about the importance of adopting the research procedures." In a discussion, clearly state your point of view and give reasons. "We will decide first on how to enhance our study forum since doing so will benefit students significantly."
- Use appropriate signposts to indicate changes in topic or point of view. For example, "Now let's go on to the next point." or "That may be true. However, …."

➤ **Listeners' needs**
- Make your point or goals clear from the beginning, so that your listeners understand your purpose for speaking. For example, "I'd like to discuss the plans for the research project."
- Give clear signposts so that your listeners can follow what is being presented or discussed. For example, "I am going to present three options for development." or "Let's compare the past with the present."
- Check your listeners' reactions to ensure that they can understand your pronunciation, word stress and intonation. Watch their facial expressions or listen for clarification requests.
- Give your listeners opportunities to interrupt or clarify to ensure correct understanding. For example, "Do you have any questions?", "Docs that make sense?" or "Is that clear?"

➤ **Fluency and cohesion**
- Pronounce words and expressions intelligibly, with appropriate stress, intonation and attention to the articulation of word endings. For example, pronounce the ending "s" clearly in "The students need to have copies of all documents."
- Link ideas appropriately, using linking words and expressions such as "so," "because," "then" to produce a smooth flow of connected speech.

➤ **Control of language**
- Ensure the range of vocabulary and choice of words appropriately convey the intended meaning. For example, use "concerned" rather than "upset" to convey that someone has raised a possible problem, rather than an immediate problem.
- Use a variety of expressions to make your speech interesting. For example, use the synonyms "tired" and "exhausted" to express the different degrees of tiredness.
- Use correct grammatical forms and structures to convey the intended meaning. For example, use the correct tenses in complex structures such as "The head of research asked whether the transcripts had been updated in the database."

➤ **Strategies**

- **Use appropriate register for the situation.** For example, use "kids" when talking informally with a friend or classmate, but use "children" when formally discussing a plan for educational sponsorship.
- **Follow appropriate turn-taking conventions** for interrupting, volunteering information or changing the subject without causing offence. For example, say "Excuse me, can I add something?" to interrupt and add information.
- **Use tentative expressions appropriately to convey politeness.** For example, say "Yes, thank you. I'd like…" instead of "Yes, I want…." as a response to "Would you like something to drink?"
- **Use clarification techniques to ensure understanding.** For example, "I'm sorry, what was that figure?" or "Can I just check that …"
- **Use appropriate intonation and stress patterns to convey feelings and views.** For example, stress the word "extremely" in "This is extremely important" for emphasis.

Understanding your strengths and weaknesses

Improving your speaking skills starts with an understanding of your own strengths and weaknesses. This will allow you to concentrate on the areas which need to be improved in general, or specifically as preparation for taking PTE Academic. Use the checklist below to assess your current speaking skills and to decide on priority areas for improvement.

Effective speaking	My current proficiency level			Priority for improvement
	High	Medium	Low	
Organization				
I can state my purpose clearly, whether in an informal or formal situation.				
I can use signposts to indicate a change in topic or point of view.				
Listeners' needs				
I can make my point or goals clear from the beginning.				
I give clear signposts to help my listeners follow what I am presenting or discussing.				
I pay attention to my listeners' reactions to check understanding in face-to-face communication.				
I pause between points to give my listeners a chance to interrupt or clarify.				

Effective speaking	My current proficiency level			Priority for improvement
	High	Medium	Low	
Fluency and cohesion				
I can use a dictionary to learn the pronunciation of unfamiliar words and the correct word stress.				
I pay attention to all aspects of pronunciation, including the endings of words.				
I can apply stress and intonation effectively to convey meaning.				
I can link my ideas with appropriate linking words and expressions.				
Control of language				
I can choose appropriate words and expressions to convey the intended meaning.				
I can use different expressions to make my speech interesting.				
I can use different verb tenses and forms correctly to convey the intended meaning.				
I can use a range of grammatical structures correctly.				
Strategies				
I understand the difference between informal and formal speech and can adjust my language accordingly.				
I have a range of expressions to use when I want to take my turn in a conversation, or interrupt a discussion to add my point of view.				
I understand and can use expressions which convey politeness.				
I know the appropriate expressions for checking and clarifying information and can use them when I need to.				
I can use appropriate intonation and stress patterns to convey feelings and views.				

3

Speaking

Developing your speaking skills

Follow the suggestions below to improve your general speaking skills.

➤ **Speak more. Look for opportunities to speak English.**

- Take an online or classroom-based speaking course. This will allow you to get speaking practice that is tailored to your proficiency level and needs.

- Join English speaking clubs either online or in your community, and get involved in the activities.
- Join special interest groups in your community that have English-speaking members, for example, theatrical societies or sports groups.
- Join or set up an English-speaking community in your area with friends or colleagues and organize English speaking social events. Choose activities for each session and make it a rule that only English is spoken.
- Sign up to online English forums that focus on topics that you are interested in.
- Invite friends or colleagues to have debates on different topics in English, for example, current affairs. Prepare points to discuss.
- Learn some English songs. For example, use the lyrics pages on a CD booklet or from the Internet to practice reading and singing a popular song. Or join some friends for an English karaoke session.
- Call in to your local English radio stations during call-in programs to express your opinions or ask questions.
- Travel to a country where English is widely spoken. This will provide an opportunity to use English for a number of different purposes in authentic contexts.

➤ **Practice pronunciation, word stress and intonation.**
- Listen to short audio recordings with transcripts. Listen again and read the transcripts of the recordings aloud together with the speakers.
- Read aloud the dialogues in novels or short stories to dramatize the stories. Aim to express the feelings of the characters as you read, using appropriate stress and intonation.
- Read simple poems and rhymes to improve your pronunciation and rhythm. Exaggerate your speaking performance to have some fun and enhance your pronunciation.

➤ **Develop a checklist of useful words, expressions and structures.**
- Keep a record of useful words and phrases that you hear or read. Note these words and expressions, with the meaning, in a place where they are easily accessible. Refer to them regularly, aiming to memorize and use them appropriately when you speak.
- Use a dictionary to check the pronunciation and stress of the words that you are not sure of.
- Use a thesaurus to find synonyms for common words, so that you can increase your range of expressions. Check back with a dictionary to ensure that you understand any specific differences between the original word and its synonyms.
- Improve the accuracy of your use of grammatical structures. Make a list of the structures you want to improve and look for information and practice materials in grammar books or on the Internet.

➤ **Read more.**
- Read English in different formats, such as short stories, novels, magazine or e-zine articles, blogs and so on. This will expand your range of English expressions and your knowledge of conventions in speaking.
- Refer to "Sources of reading material" in the section "Improving general reading skills" in Chapter 5 of the *Official Guide* for other useful reading materials.

Speaking strategies

➤ **Be prepared to start a conversation.**

- Use conventional openings in different situations. For example, in a formal situation such as attending a meeting with people you do not know well, introduce yourself by saying "How do you do?" or "Hello, how are you?"

➤ **Keep the conversation going.**

- Ask questions, but not as if you are interrogating the person. For example, asking a lot of personal questions such as "Where do you live?", "Are you married?", "How many children do you have?", "What is your job?", "Do you like it here?" one after the other, can make other people feel very uncomfortable. Instead, comment on what the person has told you or ask a little more about what they have said. For example, if someone says they live in a particular country, you could ask what they think you should see if you visit that area.
- Elaborate a little to add information or extend the discussion. For example, if someone asks you how you got to the meeting, you might say "I took the bus." Then follow up with a comment about the convenience of public transportation.

➤ **Use verbal and non-verbal strategies.**

- Pay attention to other people's body language, including facial expressions and gestures. These will help you determine what they are thinking and feeling.
- Use clarification techniques to check your understanding or ask for repetition of the information you have missed. For example, "I'm sorry, I didn't quite catch that.", "I'm not sure that I understand" or "Can I check again—when will we meet next week?"

➤ **Prepare for formal presentations.**

- Rehearse presentations so that you feel confident. Memorize your opening and closing sections to start and end fluently.
- Use signposting phrases to indicate changes in topic. For example, "Now I'll move on to … ."
- Think of questions that you might be asked, and try answering the questions by speaking aloud to yourself.

Sources of spoken English

- Online English courses or textbooks with accompanying CDs or DVDs provide samples of authentic or adapted spoken English. These courses or textbooks often provide speaking practice activities or grammar practice exercises.
- English-speaking groups offer the opportunity to practice both speaking and listening skills. Search for global groups on the Internet and find out about local clubs in your area.
- The Internet offers the opportunity to listen to a wide range of spoken English including presentations, lectures, descriptions, stories, commentaries and more.
- Television programs offer a range of situations in which authentic and scripted language is used. Some programs are subtitled, which can be helpful for overall comprehension and for exposure to a wide range of topics and language.

3

Speaking

- Radio broadcasts provide samples of spoken English on a wide range of topics. News broadcasts provide exposure to short, well-organized presentations on a number of topics. Stories provide samples of character description and dialogue.
- Face-to-face public lectures or short talks are usually well-structured and are sometimes accompanied by written outlines, which can be helpful for both listening and speaking practice.

Preparing for PTE Academic

To prepare for PTE Academic, you should practice the speaking skills that you will be assessed on in the test:

- Read Chapter 3 of the *Official Guide* to obtain information on all aspects of the speaking item types in the test and practice responding to the example items.
- Use the CD-ROM included with the *Official Guide* to gain further practice in responding to speaking items.
- Use the PTE Academic Tutorial available at www.pearsonpte.com to learn how to respond to these items in the actual test.
- Take a practice test available at www.pearsonpte.com.

Refer to the section "Resources" in Chapter 2 of the *Official Guide* for further information.

PTE Academic

Writing

Sections 3–6 of the speaking and writing part of PTE Academic (Part 1) test your ability to produce written English in an academic environment.

Part 1: Speaking and writing		
Section	Item type	Time allowed
Section 1	Personal introduction	1 minute
Section 2	Read aloud	30–35 minutes
	Repeat sentence	
	Describe image	
	Re-tell lecture	
	Answer short question	
Sections 3–4	Summarize written text	20 minutes
Section 5	Summarize written text or Write essay	10 or 20 minutes
Section 6	Write essay	20 minutes

Writing skills

The writing skills tested in PTE Academic include the following:

- writing for a purpose (to learn, to inform, to persuade)
- supporting an opinion with details, examples and explanations

- organizing sentences and paragraphs in a logical way
- developing complex ideas within a complete essay
- writing a summary
- writing under timed conditions
- using correct grammar, spelling, mechanics and words and phrases appropriate to the context
- taking notes while reading a text
- taking notes while listening to a recording (in Part 3 Listening)
- synthesizing information
- writing from dictation (in Part 3 Listening)
- writing to meet strict length requirements
- communicating the main points of a reading passage in writing
- communicating the main points of a lecture in writing (in Part 3 Listening)

Overview

Writing item types require you to write a response in standard academic English using correct grammar and spelling. PTE Academic recognizes English spelling conventions from the United States, the United Kingdom, Australia and Canada. However, one spelling convention should be used consistently in a given response.

Two item types appear in the writing sections of PTE Academic. The total time to complete the writing sections is 40, 50 or 60 minutes, depending on the combination of items in a given test. You could be required to write two summaries and one essay (40 minutes), three summaries and one essay (50 minutes), or two summaries and two essays (60 minutes). *Summarize written text* is an integrated item type that assesses both writing and reading skills.

Sections 3–6 (writing) total time: 40, 50 or 60 minutes					
Item type	Task	Skills assessed	Text/Prompt length	Response length	Time to answer
Summarize written text	After reading a passage, write a one-sentence summary of the passage.	reading and writing	text up to 300 words	one sentence 5–75 words	10 minutes
Write essay	Write an essay of 200–300 words on a given topic.	writing	up to 4 sentences	200–300 words	20 minutes

Authentic passages for the item type *Summarize written text* about academic subjects in the humanities, natural sciences or social sciences are presented. You may not be familiar with the topics presented but all the information you need is contained in the passages.

You may take notes using the Erasable Noteboard Booklet and pen, and use these notes as a guide when answering the items.

Writing item types are timed individually. You can refer to the timer in the upper right hand corner of the computer screen, "Time Remaining," which counts down the time remaining for each item.

Summarize written text

Task

Summarize written text is a short-answer writing item type. It tests your ability to comprehend, analyze and combine information from a reading passage, and then summarize the key points in writing. It assesses both writing and reading skills. The image below shows the item type.

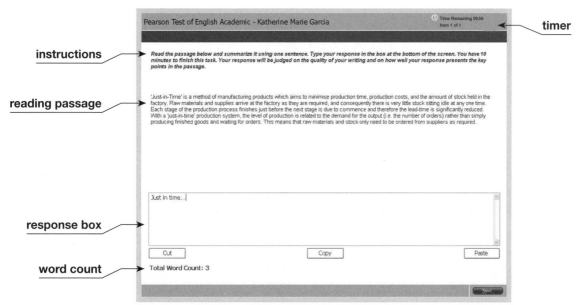

PTE Academic: Summarize written text

Below are the features of *Summarize written text*.

1 Instructions are presented at the top of the computer screen.

> *Read the passage below and summarize it using one sentence. Type your response in the box at the bottom of the screen. You have 10 minutes to finish this task. Your response will be judged on the quality of your writing and on how well your response presents the key points in the passage.*

2 A reading passage follows.

> 'Just-in-Time' is a method of manufacturing products which aims to minimise production time, production costs, and the amount of stock held in the factory. Raw materials and supplies arrive at the factory as they are required, and consequently there is very little stock sitting idle at any one time. Each stage of the production process finishes just before the next stage is due to commence and therefore the lead-time is significantly reduced. With a 'Just-in-Time' production system, the level of production is related to the demand for the output (i.e. the number of orders) rather than simply producing finished goods and waiting for orders. This means that raw materials and stock only need to be ordered from suppliers as required.

3 A response box follows.

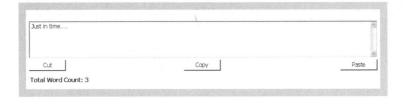

Use this space to type your summary. You can select text within the response box with the mouse, and use the "Cut," "Copy" and "Paste" buttons to edit your response. The "Total Word Count" keeps track of the number of words written and updates as you type.

4 The timer will count down from 10 minutes for this item type. Click on the "Next" button to go to the next item.

The reading passages for this item type are up to 300 words in length. There are two to three *Summarize written text* items in PTE Academic, depending on the combination of items in a given test. They are presented together in a single block. This item type is individually timed. You have 10 minutes to answer each *Summarize written text* item. After 10 minutes, the test will automatically move on to the next item.

> No test taker will be presented with a combination of the maximum number of items for the two writing item types *Summarize written text* (three) and *Write Essay* (two). The maximum number possible in any given test is four writing items.

Scoring

Your response for *Summarize written text* is judged on the quality of your writing and on how well your response presents the key points in the passage. Your score is based on four factors:

➤ **Content:** Does your response summarize the main points in the passage?

Content is scored by determining if all key points of the passage have been addressed without misrepresenting the purpose or topic. If your summary misinterprets the topic or the purpose of the passage, you will not receive any score points for your summary on any of the four factors. Your summary will be scored zero. The best responses clearly summarize the main idea and condense essential supporting points. They focus on the topic, including only key information and essential supporting points.

➤ **Form:** Does your response meet the requirements of a one-sentence summary? If your summary contains fewer than five words or more than 75 words, you will not receive any score points for your summary on any of the four factors. Your summary will be scored zero.

➤ **Grammar:** Does your response demonstrate correct grammatical usage?

Grammar is scored by determining if the basic structure of the sentence is correct. The best responses usually consist of a main clause and subordinate clause.

➤ **Vocabulary:** Does your response demonstrate correct and appropriate word choice and usage?

Vocabulary is scored according to its relevance to the passage and its appropriateness in an academic environment. The appropriate use of synonyms is also scored. The best responses use words from the passage appropriately, demonstrate an understanding of the context and use synonyms effectively to show variety in language use.

Partial credit scoring applies to *Summarize written text*. No credit is given for no response or an irrelevant response. This item type affects the scoring of the following:

Overall score	✔		
Communicative skills			
Listening		Speaking	
Reading	✔	Writing	✔
Enabling skills			
Grammar	✔	Spelling	
Oral fluency		Vocabulary	✔
Pronunciation		Written discourse	

Reading and writing skills

Summarize written text is an integrated skills item type that tests both your reading and writing skills in an academic environment. The key skills tested are on the next page.

Reading

- reading a passage under timed conditions
- identifying a writer's purpose, style, tone, or attitude
- comprehending explicit and implicit information
- comprehending concrete and abstract information

Writing

- writing a summary
- writing under timed conditions
- taking notes while reading a text
- synthesizing information
- writing to meet strict length requirements
- communicating the main points of a reading passage in writing
- using words and phrases appropriate to the context
- using correct grammar
- using correct spelling

Your listening and speaking skills are not tested by this item type.

Strategies

Before writing

- Read the passage carefully, focusing on the content. Try to infer the meaning of any unknown words and phrases.
- Re-read the passage and take note of the topic sentences and key words if necessary.

While writing

- Focus on the key words. Your summary should include the main ideas presented in the passage. These are usually indicated in the topic sentences.
- Do not include background knowledge or your own ideas. Remember that all of the information you need to write your summary is contained in the passage.
- Do not refer back to the passage in your summary. Imagine that you have to do this for a person who has not seen the passage.
- Use grammatical structures that you feel confident about. You will make fewer mistakes.

After writing

- Check the content of your summary.

  — Does it convey the main ideas in the passage?
  — Does it include essential supporting points?

- Check the length of your summary.

  — Is it expressed in one single complete sentence? Do not write more than one sentence.
  — How many words does the sentence contain? Do not use more than 75 words or fewer than five words.

- Check grammar, spelling and punctuation, and make corrections where necessary.

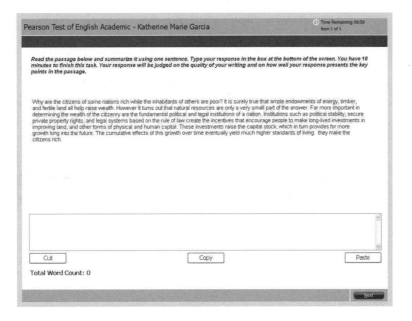

Practice

Below is a *Summarize written text* item for you to respond to.

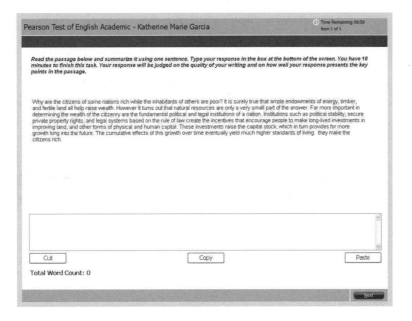

10 min. **Read the passage. Then summarize it using one sentence. Write your response in the space provided below. To simulate the test conditions, give yourself only 10 minutes to respond to this item.**

> Why are the citizens of some nations rich while the inhabitants of others are poor? It is surely true that ample endowments of energy, timber, and fertile land all help raise wealth. However it turns out that natural resources are only a very small part of the answer. Far more important in determining the wealth of the citizenry are the fundamental political and legal institutions of a nation. Institutions such as political stability, secure private property rights, and legal systems based on the rule of law create the incentives that encourage people to make long-lived investments in improving land, and other forms of physical and human capital. These investments raise the capital stock, which in turn provides for more growth long into the future. The cumulative effects of this growth over time eventually yield much higher standards of living: they make the citizens rich.

Remember, during PTE Academic you will type in your response at a test delivery workstation.

4

Writing

Answer key **p.178** **Now check the Answer key.**

Write essay

Task

Write essay is a long-answer writing item type. It tests your ability to write a persuasive or argumentative essay on a given topic. It assesses writing skills. The image below shows the item type.

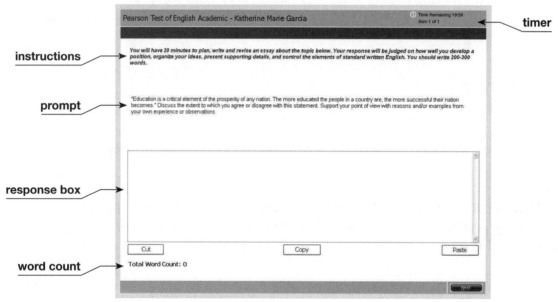

PTE Academic: Write essay

Below are the features of *Write essay*.

1 Instructions are presented at the top of the computer screen.

> *You will have 20 minutes to plan, write and revise an essay about the topic below. Your response will be judged on how well you develop a position, organize your ideas, present supporting details, and control the elements of standard written English. You should write 200–300 words.*

2 A prompt follows.

> "Education is a critical element to the prosperity of any nation. The more educated the people in a country are, the more successful their nation becomes." Discuss the extent to which you agree or disagree with this statement. Support your point of view with reasons and/or examples from your own experience or observations.

3 A response box follows.

Use this space to type your essay. You can select text within the response box with the mouse, and use the "Cut," "Copy" and "Paste" buttons to edit your response. The "Total Word Count" keeps track of the number of words written and updates as you type.

4 The timer will count down from 20 minutes for this item type. Click on the "Next" button to go to the next item.

There are one to two *Write essay* items in PTE Academic, depending on the combination of items in a given test. They are presented in a single block. This item type is individually timed. You have 20 minutes to answer each *Write essay* item. After 20 minutes, the test will automatically move on to the next item.

> No test taker will be presented with a combination of the maximum number of items for the two writing item types *Write Essay* (two) and *Summarize written text* (three). The maximum number possible in any given test is four writing items.

Scoring

Your score on *Write essay* is based on seven factors:

➤ **Content:** Does your response address the topic?

Content is scored by determining if all aspects of the topic have been addressed in your response. The appropriateness of the details, examples and explanations used to support your point of view is also scored. If your essay does not address the topic, you will not receive any score points for your essay on any of the seven factors. Your essay will be scored zero. The best responses are on topic, contain logical and specific information and answer any questions asked. They also support any arguments with details, examples and/or explanations.

➤ **Development, structure and coherence:** Does your response demonstrate good development of ideas and a logical structure?

Development, structure and coherence are scored according to the organization of your response. A well-developed response uses a logical organizational pattern, connects ideas and

4

Writing

79

explains these connections. The best responses contain multiple paragraphs and have a clear introduction, body and conclusion that relate to the topic of the essay. Within paragraphs, ideas are clearly presented and supported with details, examples and/or explanations. Transitions between paragraphs are smooth.

➤ **Form:** Does your response meet the length requirement of between 200 and 300 words?

Form is scored by counting the number of words in your response. You will receive full credit if your essay is between 200 and 300 words. Writing less than 200 words or more than 300 words will decrease your score. If your essay contains less than 120 words or more than 380 words, you will not receive any score points for your essay on any of the seven factors. Your essay will be scored zero.

➤ **General linguistic range:** Does your response use language that precisely conveys your ideas?

General linguistic range is scored by determining if the language in your response accurately communicates your ideas. This includes your ability to provide clear descriptions, change emphasis, eliminate ambiguity, express subtleties in meaning, and use stylistic features to communicate meaning. You are more likely to receive full credit if you use complex sentence structures and vocabulary correctly, rather than consistently using simple sentence structures and vocabulary. This is because complex ideas are often expressed with complex sentence structures and vocabulary. The best responses use language that highlights key ideas, creatively expresses opinions and ensures clear communication.

➤ **Grammar usage and mechanics:** Does your response demonstrate correct grammatical usage and consistent control of standard written English?

Grammar usage and mechanics are scored by examining sentence structure, punctuation and capitalization. The best responses contain high proportions of grammatically correct complex sentences that clearly communicate the intended meaning.

➤ **Vocabulary range:** Does your response demonstrate command of a broad vocabulary range?

Vocabulary range is scored according to the variety of words in your response and their appropriateness in an academic environment. Synonyms, idiomatic expressions and academic terms are also assessed if appropriate. The best responses use precise academic terms and avoid repetition by using synonyms and idioms where appropriate.

➤ **Spelling:** Does your response demonstrate correct and consistent use of a single spelling convention?

PTE Academic recognizes English spelling conventions from the United States, the United Kingdom, Australia and Canada. However, one spelling convention should be used consistently in a given response.

Partial credit scoring applies to *Write essay*. No credit is given for no response or an irrelevant response. This item type affects the scoring of the following:

Overall score			✔
Communicative skills			
Listening		Speaking	
Reading		Writing	✔
Enabling skills			
Grammar	✔	Spelling	✔
Oral fluency		Vocabulary	✔
Pronunciation		Written discourse	✔

Writing skills

Write essay tests your writing skills in an academic environment. Below are the key skills tested:

- writing for a purpose (to learn, to inform, to persuade)
- supporting an opinion with details, examples and explanations
- organizing sentences and paragraphs in a logical way
- developing complex ideas within a complete essay
- using words and phrases appropriate to the context
- using correct grammar
- using correct spelling
- using correct mechanics
- writing under timed conditions

Your listening and speaking skills are not tested by this item type, and your reading skills are only used to read the instructions and the prompt.

Strategies

Before writing

- Read the essay prompt carefully. Consider exactly what the requirements of the essay are. For example, you may have to do one or more of the following:

    — Agree or disagree with a statement.
    — Argue for or against an opinion.
    — Describe a situation.
    — Answer a question.
    — Discuss advantages or disadvantages.

    If your writing fails to meet any one of the requirements of the essay, your score will be affected. If you write about something other than the topic presented in the prompt, your essay will be scored zero.

- Plan the content of your essay using the Erasable Noteboard Booklet and pen:
  — Note any helpful ideas, phrases or words.
  — Organize your ideas into groups.
  — Sequence your ideas.
  — Check your plan against the essay prompt.

- Check the timer. Plan how much time you will use to write, allowing a few minutes at the end for revising and proofreading.

While writing

- Write quickly, referring to your plan when necessary.
- Check the word count as you write.

After writing

- Read your essay and consider how effective it is:
  — Is the content relevant to the topic given?
  — Would the ideas and the way they are developed be clear to another reader?
  — Is there an introduction to the topic?
  — Is there a clear conclusion?
  — Are new ideas introduced in separate paragraphs?
  — Are the connections between sentences and paragraphs clear?
  — Have a variety of words or phrases been used when referring to the same subject?
  — Could the choice of words or phrases be improved?

- Check the total word count. It should be between 200 and 300 words. If it is not, adjust the text length accordingly.

- Check the grammar, spelling and punctuation, and make corrections where necessary.

Practice

Below is a *Write essay* item for you to respond to.

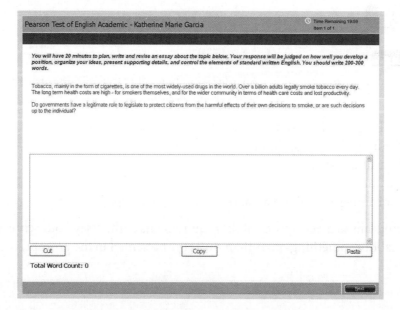

20 min. **Read the topic. Then write an essay about the topic in the space provided below. You should write 200–300 words. To simulate the test conditions, give yourself only 20 minutes to plan and respond to this item.**

Tobacco, mainly in the form of cigarettes, is one of the most widely-used drugs in the world. Over a billion adults legally smoke tobacco every day. The long term health costs are high—for smokers themselves, and for the wider community in terms of health care costs and lost productivity.

Do governments have a legitimate role to legislate to protect citizens from the harmful effects of their own decisions to smoke, or are such decisions up to the individual?

Remember, during PTE Academic you will type in your response at a test delivery workstation.

4

Writing

Answer key p.178 **Now check the Answer key.**

Improving general writing skills

Effective writing

Effective writing, in both everyday and test situations, requires attention to the three areas listed below. Although not all of these areas will be tested in PTE Academic, improving your skills in each area will help your general language proficiency and improve your overall performance in the test.

➤ **Organization**
- State the purpose clearly. For example, "This report recommends the use of a new computer program."
- Use topic sentences to convey the key ideas.
- Arrange the sections, paragraphs and information in a logical order. For example, follow a sequence of introduction, body text and conclusion.
- Use signposting words such as "first," "second," "finally" to indicate the overall organization and coherence of your writing.
- Follow different structural conventions for different types of writing. For example, include sub-headings in a report.

➤ **Readers' needs**
- Think about what the target readers already know and what they need to know. Include all necessary information. For example, in an academic report, include the necessary background information to help readers understand what will be discussed.
- Indicate your purpose at the beginning. For example, state what you will do or what argument and/or message you will put forward.
- Arrange ideas or information in a way that is easy to follow and understand.
- Use formatting, style and register that are appropriate for the target readers. Follow standard conventions for a specific genre.

➤ **Control of language**
- Ensure the range of vocabulary and choice of words are appropriate to the context and convey the intended meaning. For example, when describing a reputable university, use "well-known" instead of "famous."
- Use different forms of expression to make your writing interesting. For example, "We need to consider this program because it will increase revenue," or "We should think about the increased revenue that this program can produce."
- Use verb tenses correctly to reflect the intended times of and connections between events. For example, "Work on the study had only just started when the head of research resigned." This indicates that the head of research left the study soon after the work began.
- Use grammatical structures correctly to construct complete sentences and to build connections between ideas. For example, "While we were searching for a solution" is not a complete sentence because the information is dependent on additional detail that has not been included. The idea needs to be constructed as "We found a possible answer while

we were searching for a solution." The cause and effect relationship is clear in the sentence "Results were delayed because of problems with the database."

- Use punctuation and spelling correctly to enhance the readers' understanding.

Understanding your strengths and weaknesses

Improving your writing skills starts with an understanding of your own strengths and weaknesses. This will allow you to concentrate on the areas which need to be improved in general, or specifically as preparation for taking PTE Academic. Use the checklist below to assess your current writing skills and to decide on priority areas for improvement.

Effective writing	My current proficiency level			Priority for improvement
	High	Medium	Low	
Organization				
I make sure my purpose is clearly stated.				
I use topic sentences to convey key ideas.				
I can arrange the sections, paragraphs and information in a logical order.				
I can use signposting words to indicate the overall organization and coherence of my writing.				
I can use appropriate and standard structural conventions for different types of writing.				
Readers' needs				
I think about what my readers already know and what they need to know and include all necessary information.				
I state the purpose of the writing at the beginning.				
I can arrange ideas or information in a way that is easy to follow and understand.				
I follow normal organizational and language conventions for specific types of writing.				
Control of language				
I can use appropriate words and expressions to express the intended meaning.				
I can describe similar ideas in more than one way.				
I can use verb tenses correctly to reflect the intended times of and connections between events.				
I can use grammatical structures correctly to construct complete sentences and to build connections between ideas.				
I can spell words correctly.				
I can use common punctuation conventions.				

4

Writing

Developing your writing skills

Follow the suggestions below to improve your general writing skills.

➤ **Read more.**
- Read for pleasure and interest to build your language appreciation and knowledge.
- Develop a habit of reading in English to become familiar with effective expressions in writing.

  — Locate and read different types of texts, such as news reports, short stories, editorials, descriptions of places or trips, news about scientific inventions, or the development of new technology.
  — Notice how the text is organized—main idea and examples, arguments for and against, past vs. present vs. future, eye-catching headline followed by facts, etc.
  — Ask yourself what the purpose of the text is.
  — Note words and expressions that are useful for topics that you may write about.
  — Find and review sentences or phrases that show connections between different ideas.
  — Check how the text ends. How does the writer reach a conclusion? What words or expressions are used to end the text?

➤ **Practice writing. Take every opportunity to write in English.**
- Write emails and text messages in English. Exchange information with English-speaking friends or contacts.
- Keep a journal. Write about your feelings and describe the events that happen. Explain your views about different topics.
- Write about a topic under timed conditions. Choose a topic and set a time limit. Write as much as you can within the time limit. Then ask yourself what was most challenging—planning what to write, finding something to write about, writing enough words, getting your ideas conveyed within the time limit, or allocating time for planning and review. Practice again, focusing on the areas you found challenging and trying to improve your effectiveness each time you write.
- Obtain feedback and revise. Show what you write to English-speaking teachers or friends for comments. Use their feedback to revise your writing.
- Take an online or classroom-based writing course. This will allow you to get writing practice that is tailored to your proficiency level and needs.

➤ **Develop an editing checklist for the areas that you need to improve, such as grammatical structures and vocabulary.**
- Note what you need to pay attention to and improve. For example, you may need to practice more on parts of speech, or subject-verb agreement. Add these items to your editing checklist under a heading, for example, "Grammar."
- List areas that you are not sure about, for example, when to use "confidence" or "confident." Check with a textbook, the Internet, or ask a teacher or friend to find out the answers. Make notes in your editing checklist.
- Use the "spellcheck" function when you are working on a computer, and note any spelling mistakes. Ask yourself which words you are not sure how to spell. Look up the spellings and add them to your checklist.

- Add new words and phrases to your list regularly. Expand and consolidate your knowledge of the words used frequently in academic texts. You may refer to *Longman Exams Dictionary* for a list of academic words as well as lists of the most frequent words categorized by topic.
- Review your checklist regularly to strengthen specific areas of your written English.

Writing strategies

Follow a sequence of "Plan, draft, check and finalize" to write effectively.

➤ **Plan**
- Consider carefully:
  - your purpose for writing, for example, to give information, or to persuade your readers to do something.
  - the topic(s) you want to cover.
  - who the intended readers are and what they may already know about the topic(s).
- Make notes of the key ideas you want to include.
- Arrange your notes in a logical order that will effectively convey your message to your readers. Remove any ideas you decide not to use.

➤ **Draft**
- Draft your text, referring to the plan you have made. Aim to write quickly, expressing your ideas as best as you can. At this stage, try not to spend a lot of time composing each separate sentence.

➤ **Check**
- Review what you have written. Try to put yourself in the position of your readers, and mark any expressions or points which you feel are unclear, or could be improved.
- Make changes and review again.
- Check grammar, spelling and punctuation, and make corrections where necessary.

➤ **Finalize**
- Produce a final version.

Sources of written English

- The Internet includes examples of all types of writing.
- News articles, essays and reports provide good examples of organization. They often put the main point at the beginning, use topic sentences to start paragraphs and develop an argument or discussion in a logical way. As these genres generally cover a range of topics, they are good sources of vocabulary and expressions in specific subject areas. They can also provide useful examples of logical argument and the use of linking words and phrases to express relationships between ideas.
- Online English courses and textbooks provide models for different types of writing with common organizational structures and useful language.

- Academic journals in different fields of study contain articles with abstracts which summarize purpose, content and conclusions.
- Novels and short stories are useful sources of various written styles of English. They will also help to increase your vocabulary.

Preparing for PTE Academic

To prepare for PTE Academic, you should practice the writing skills that you will be assessed on in the test:

- Read Chapter 4 of the *Official Guide* to obtain information on all aspects of the writing item types in the test and practice responding to the example items.
- Use the CD-ROM included with the *Official Guide* to gain further practice in responding to writing items.
- Use the PTE Academic Tutorial available at www.pearsonpte.com to learn how to respond to these items in the actual test.
- Take a practice test available at www.pearsonpte.com.

Refer to the section "Resources" in Chapter 2 of the *Official Guide* for further information.

PTE Academic

Reading

Part 2: Reading of PTE Academic tests your ability to understand written English in an academic environment.

Reading skills

The reading skills tested in PTE Academic include the following:

- identifying the topic, theme or main ideas
- identifying supporting points or examples
- identifying words and phrases appropriate to the context
- identifying a writer's purpose, style, tone, or attitude
- identifying the relationships between sentences and paragraphs
- understanding academic vocabulary
- understanding the difference between connotation and denotation
- inferring the meaning of unfamiliar words
- comprehending explicit and implicit information
- comprehending concrete and abstract information
- classifying and categorizing information
- following a logical or chronological sequence of events
- evaluating the quality and usefulness of texts
- reading a text under timed conditions
- evaluating and synthesizing information
- reading for information to infer meanings or find relationships
- reading for overall organization and connections between pieces of information

- identifying specific details, facts, opinions, definitions or sequences of events
- identifying the most accurate summary (in Part 3 Listening)
- matching written text to speech (in Part 3 Listening)

Overview

Reading item types require you to understand an authentic text from an academic source.

Five item types appear in the reading part of PTE Academic. The total time to complete the reading part of the test is approximately 32–41 minutes, depending on the combination of items in a given test. *Reading & writing: Fill in the blanks* is an integrated item type that assesses both reading and writing skills.

Part 2 (reading) total time: 32–41 minutes			
Item type	Task	Skills assessed	Text length
Multiple-choice, choose single answer	After reading a text, answer a multiple-choice question on the content or tone of the text by selecting one response.	reading	text up to 300 words
Multiple-choice, choose multiple answers	After reading a text, answer a multiple-choice question on the content or tone of the text by selecting more than one response.	reading	text up to 300 words
Re-order paragraphs	Several text boxes appear on screen in random order. Put the text boxes in the correct order.	reading	text up to 150 words
Reading: Fill in the blanks	A text appears on screen with several blanks. Drag words or phrases from the blue box to fill in the blanks.	reading	text up to 80 words
Reading & writing: Fill in the blanks	A text appears on screen with several blanks. Fill in the blanks by selecting words from several drop down lists of response options.	reading and writing	text up to 300 words

Authentic texts about academic subjects in the humanities, natural sciences or social sciences are presented. Although you may not be familiar with the topics presented, all the information you need to answer the items is contained in the texts.

You may take notes using the Erasable Noteboard Booklet and pen, and use these notes as a guide when answering the items.

Reading item types are not timed individually. You can refer to the timer in the upper right hand corner of the computer screen, "Time Remaining," which counts down the time remaining for the reading part.

Multiple-choice, choose single answer

Task

Multiple-choice, choose single answer is a multiple-choice reading item type with a single correct response. It tests your ability to analyze, interpret and evaluate a short reading text on an academic subject. It assesses reading skills. The image below shows the item type.

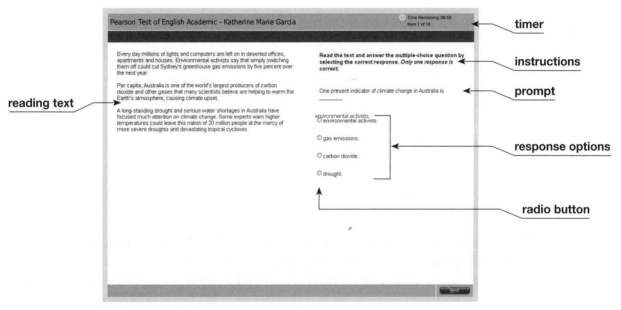

PTE Academic: Multiple-choice, choose single answer

Below are the features of *Multiple-choice, choose single answer*.

1 Instructions are presented at the top right side of the computer screen.

> *Read the text and answer the multiple-choice question by selecting the correct response. Only one response is correct.*

2 A reading text is presented on the left side.

Every day millions of lights and computers are left on in deserted offices, apartments and houses. Environmental activists say that simply switching them off could cut Sydney's greenhouse gas emissions by five percent over the next year.

Per capita, Australia is one of the world's largest producers of carbon dioxide and other gases that many scientists believe are helping to warm the Earth's atmosphere, causing climate upset.

A long-standing drought and serious water shortages in Australia have focused much attention on climate change. Some experts warn higher temperatures could leave this nation of 20 million people at the mercy of more severe droughts and devastating tropical cyclones.

3 A prompt with three to five response options follows the instructions.

One present indicator of climate change in Australia is _____

○ environmental activists.

○ gas emissions.

○ carbon dioxide.

○ drought.

To select a response, click on the corresponding radio button or the response itself. Your response will be highlighted in yellow. To deselect your response, click on the radio button or the response again. To change your response, click on a different radio button or a different response.

4 Click on the "Next" button to go to the next item. The timer for the reading part will continue running.

The reading texts for this item type are up to 300 words in length. There are two to three *Multiple-choice, choose single answer* items in the reading part of PTE Academic, depending on the combination of items in a given test. They are presented together in a single block.

Scoring

Your response is scored as either correct or incorrect. No credit is given for no response or an incorrect response. This item type affects the scoring of the following:

Overall score	✔		
Communicative skills			
Listening		Speaking	
Reading	✔	Writing	
Enabling skills			
Grammar		Spelling	
Oral fluency		Vocabulary	
Pronunciation		Written discourse	

Reading skills

Multiple-choice, choose single answer tests your reading skills in an academic environment. Any of the following reading skills could be tested by this item type:

➤ **Main idea or gist:** Read for and identify the main idea or theme of the text. For example, "What is the central focus of the text?"

➤ **Detailed information:** Read for and identify specific details, facts, opinions, definitions or sequences of events. For example, "According to the text, which of the following contributed to young people joining the movement?"

➤ **Writer's purpose:** Read for and understand the function of what the writer says, or identify the reasons why the writer mentions specific pieces of information. For example, "What does the writer seek to achieve in the text?"

➤ **Organization:** Read for and identify the overall organization and connections between pieces of information. This evaluates your ability to link different parts of the text together. For example, "What do the first sentence and third paragraph have in common?"

➤ **Inference:** Read a text and infer meanings, form, generalizations, make predictions, find relationships or draw conclusions. For example, "What conclusion about the monarchy can be drawn from the arguments presented in the text?"

➤ **Textual value:** Read for and assess the quality and usefulness of the text. For example, "Which of the following statements leads you to question the reliability of the information presented by the writer?"

5

Reading

➤ **Stylistics:** Read for and identify the writer's attitude, feelings or degree of certainty on an issue. For example, "In line five the writer uses the word 'guy.' What do you think is the reason for this?"

Your listening, speaking and writing skills are not tested by this item type.

Strategies

Before reading

- Read the prompt carefully. This will help you understand what to read for.
- Skim the response options quickly.

While reading

- Read the whole text carefully.
- Identify the main idea and supporting points.
- Do not focus too much on unfamiliar words. Try to infer the meaning of these words from the context.

After reading

- Read the response options and select the correct one.

  — First eliminate any response options which you feel sure are incorrect.
  — Then select one of the remaining response options. Do not try to simply match words or phrases with those in the text. Sometimes incorrect options contain the same words as the text.

- Check your response if you are not sure.

  — If the prompt relates to a detail, find the relevant part of the text to check the response option you have chosen.
  — If the prompt relates to a more general aspect of the text, quickly re-read the text to check the response option you have chosen.

- Do not change your first response unless you feel sure that it is incorrect.
- Make a guess if you are still not sure which is the correct response. It is better to attempt to answer the item rather than leave it unanswered.

Practice

Below is a *Multiple-choice, choose single answer* item for you to respond to.

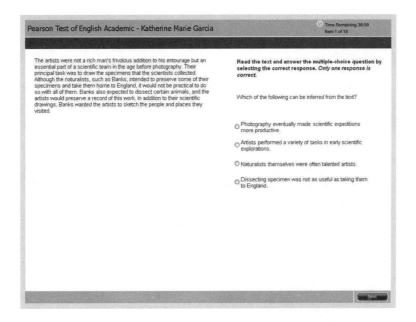

Read the prompt and the text. Then select the correct response.

The artists were not a rich man's frivolous addition to his entourage but an essential part of a scientific team in the age before photography. Their principal task was to draw the specimens that the scientists collected. Although the naturalists, such as Banks, intended to preserve some of their specimens and take them home to England, it would not be practical to do so with all of them. Banks also expected to dissect certain animals, and the artists would preserve a record of this work. In addition to their scientific drawings, Banks wanted the artists to sketch the people and places they visited.

Which of the following can be inferred from the text?

○ Photography eventually made scientific expeditions more productive.

○ Artists performed a variety of tasks in early scientific explorations.

○ Naturalists themselves were often talented artists.

○ Dissecting specimens was not as useful as taking them to England.

Remember, during PTE Academic you will give your response by clicking on a response at a test delivery workstation.

Answer key p.181 **Now check the Answer key.**

Multiple-choice, choose multiple answers

Task

Multiple-choice, choose multiple answers is a multiple-choice reading item type with more than one correct response. It tests your ability to analyze, interpret and evaluate a short reading text on an academic subject. It assesses reading skills. The image below shows the item type.

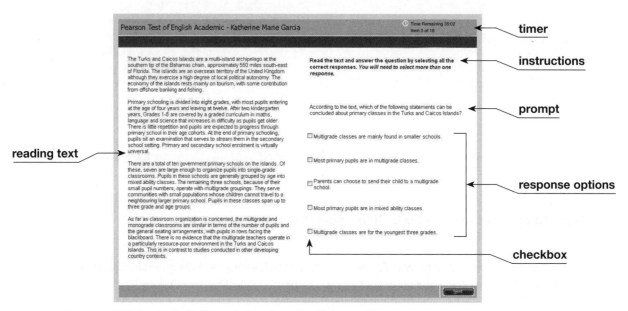

PTE Academic: Multiple-choice, choose multiple answers

Below are the features of *Multiple-choice, choose multiple answers*.

1 Instructions are presented at the top right side of the computer screen.

> *Read the text and answer the question by selecting all the correct responses. More than one response is correct.*

2 A reading text is presented on the left side.

> The Turks and Caicos Islands are a multi-island archipelago at the southern tip of the Bahamas chain, approximately 550 miles south-east of Florida. The islands are an overseas territory of the United Kingdom although they exercise a high degree of local political autonomy. The economy of the islands rests mainly on tourism, with some contribution from offshore banking and fishing.
>
> Primary schooling is divided into eight grades, with most pupils entering at the age of four years and leaving at twelve. After two kindergarten years, Grades 1–6 are covered by a graded curriculum in maths, language and science that increases in difficulty as pupils get older. There is little repetition and pupils are expected to progress through primary school in their age cohorts. At the end of primary schooling, pupils sit an examination that serves to stream them in the secondary school setting. Primary and secondary school enrolment is virtually universal.
>
> There are a total of ten government primary schools on the islands. Of these, seven are large enough to organize pupils into single-grade classrooms. Pupils in these schools are generally grouped by age into mixed ability classes. The remaining three schools, because of their small pupil numbers, operate with multigrade groupings. They serve communities with small populations whose children cannot travel to a neighboring larger primary school. Pupils in these classes span up to three grade and age groups.
>
> As far as classroom organization is concerned, the multigrade and monograde classrooms are similar in terms of the number of pupils and the general seating arrangements, with pupils in rows facing the blackboard. There is no evidence that the multigrade teachers operate in a particularly resource-poor environment in the Turks and Caicos Islands. This is in contrast to studies conducted in other developing country contexts.

3 A prompt with five to seven response options follows the instructions.

> According to the text, which of the following statements can be concluded about primary classes in the Turks and Caicos Islands?
>
> ☐ Multigrade classes are mainly found in smaller schools.
>
> ☐ Most primary pupils are in multigrade classes.
>
> ☐ Parents can choose to send their child to a multigrade school.
>
> ☐ Most primary pupils are in mixed ability classes.
>
> ☐ Multigrade classes are for the youngest three grades.

To select a response, click on the corresponding checkbox or the response itself. Your response will be highlighted in yellow. To deselect your response, click on the checkbox or the response again. To change your responses, click on a different checkbox or a different response.

4 Click on the "Next" button to go to the next item. The timer for the reading part will continue running.

5

Reading

The reading texts for this item type are up to 300 words in length. There are two to three *Multiple-choice, choose multiple answers* items in the reading part of PTE Academic, depending on the combination of items in a given test. They are presented together in a single block.

Scoring

If all response options are correct, you receive the maximum score points for this item type. If one or more response options are incorrect, partial credit scoring applies. This is the first of three item types where you can lose points if you choose any incorrect options. For any wrong options chosen 1 point is deducted, whilst correct options are given 1 point. Make sure you are confident in your choices. This item type affects the scoring of the following:

Overall score			✔
Communicative skills			
Listening		Speaking	
Reading	✔	Writing	
Enabling skills			
Grammar		Spelling	
Oral fluency		Vocabulary	
Pronunciation		Written discourse	

Reading skills

Multiple-choice, choose multiple answers tests your reading skills in an academic environment. Any of the following reading skills could be tested by this item type:

➤ **Main idea or gist:** Read for and identify the main idea or theme of the text. For example, "What are the main ideas in the text?"

➤ **Detailed information:** Read for and identify specific details, facts, opinions, definitions or sequences of events. For example, "According to the text, which of the following indicate sleep deprivation?"

➤ **Writer's purpose:** Read for and understand the function of what the writer says, or identify the reasons why the writer mentions specific pieces of information. For example, "What does the writer seek to achieve in the text?"

➤ **Organization:** Read for and identify the overall organization and connections between pieces of information. This evaluates your ability to link different parts of the text together. For example, "What are the relationships between the second and third paragraphs?"

➤ **Inference:** Read a text and infer meanings, form generalizations, make predictions, find relationships or draw conclusions. For example, "What conclusions about organic produce can be drawn from the arguments presented in the text?"

➤ **Textual value:** Read for and assess the quality and usefulness of the text. For example, "Which of the following statements leads you to question the reliability of the information presented by the writer?"

➤ **Stylistics:** Read for and identify the writer's attitude, feelings or degree of certainty on an issue. For example, "In line three the writer uses the phrase 'happy as a clam.' What do think are the reasons for this?"

Your listening, speaking and writing skills are not tested by this item type.

Strategies

Before reading

- Read the prompt carefully. This will help you understand what to read for.
- Skim the response options quickly.

While reading

- Read the whole text carefully.
- Identify the main idea and supporting points.
- Do not focus too much on unfamiliar words. Try to infer the meaning of these words from the context.

After reading

- Read the response options and select the correct ones.
  - First eliminate any response options which you feel sure are incorrect.
  - Then select all the correct responses from the remaining response options. Do not try to simply match words or phrases with those in the text. Sometimes incorrect options contain the same words as the text.
- Check your responses if you are not sure.
  - If the prompt relates to a detail, find the relevant parts of the text to check the response options you have chosen.
  - If the prompt relates to a more general aspect of the text, quickly re-read the text to check the response options you have chosen.
- Do not change your first responses unless you feel sure that they are incorrect.

5

Reading

Practice

Below is a *Multiple-choice, choose multiple answers* item for you to respond to.

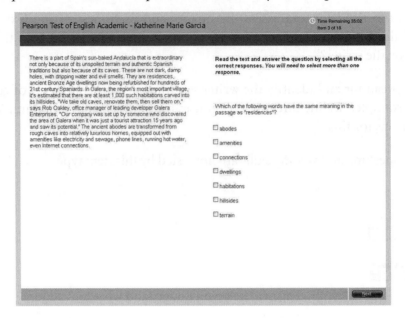

Read the prompt and the text. Then select all the correct responses.

There is a part of Spain's sun-baked Andalucía that is extraordinary not only because of its unspoiled terrain and authentic Spanish traditions but also because of its caves. These are not dark, damp holes, with dripping water and evil smells. They are residences, ancient Bronze Age dwellings now being refurbished for hundreds of 21st century Spaniards. In Galera, the region's most important village, it's estimated that there are at least 1,000 such habitations carved into its hillsides. "We take old caves, renovate them, then sell them on," says Rob Oakley, office manager of leading developer Galera Enterprises. "Our company was set up by someone who discovered the area of Galera when it was just a tourist attraction 15 years ago and saw its potential." The ancient abodes are transformed from rough caves into relatively luxurious homes, equipped out with amenities like electricity and sewage, phone lines, running hot water, even Internet connections.

Which of the following words have the same meaning in the passage as "residences"?

- ☐ abodes
- ☐ amenities
- ☐ connections
- ☐ dwellings
- ☐ habitations
- ☐ hillsides
- ☐ terrain

> Remember, during PTE Academic you will give your response by clicking on responses at a test delivery workstation.

Answer key p.182 Now check the Answer key.

Re-order paragraphs

Task

Re-order paragraphs is a reading item type with a single correct order for the text boxes in a reading text. It tests your ability to understand the organization and cohesion of an academic text. It assesses reading skills. The image below shows the item type.

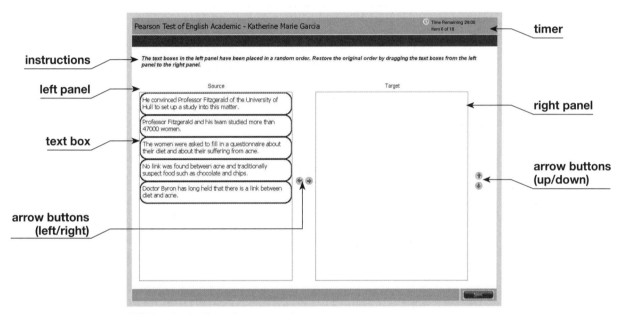

PTE Academic: Re-order paragraphs

Below are the features of *Re-order paragraphs*.

1 Instructions are presented at the top of the computer screen.

> *The text boxes in the left panel have been placed in a random order. Restore the original order by dragging the text boxes from the left panel to the right panel.*

2 The left panel, "Source," contains four or five text boxes.

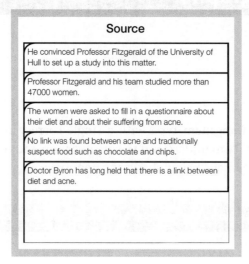

3 The right panel, "Target," is empty.

To select a text box, click on the text box. The text box will be highlighted in blue. To deselect a text box, click on another text box.

There are three ways to move a selected text box.

- Hold the left button of the mouse down and drag the text box between the panels. You can also drag text boxes within a panel.
- Click on the left/right arrow buttons to move the text box between panels. You can also use the up/down arrow buttons to re-order the text boxes in the right panel.
- Double click on a selected text box. It will move to the bottom of the opposite panel.

4 Click on the "Next" button to go to the next item. The timer for the reading part will continue running.

The reading texts for this item type are up to 150 words in length. There are two to three *Re-order paragraphs* items in PTE Academic, depending on the combination of items in a given test. They are presented together in a single block.

Scoring

If all text boxes are in the correct order, you receive the maximum score points for this item type. If one or more text boxes are in the wrong order, partial credit scoring applies. This item type affects the scoring of the following:

Overall score			✔
Communicative skills			
Listening		Speaking	
Reading	✔	Writing	
Enabling skills			
Grammar		Spelling	
Oral fluency		Vocabulary	
Pronunciation		Written discourse	

Reading skills

Re-order paragraphs tests your reading skills in an academic environment. Below are the key skills tested:

- identifying the topic, theme or main ideas
- identifying supporting points or examples
- identifying the relationships between sentences and paragraphs
- understanding academic vocabulary
- understanding the difference between connotation and denotation
- inferring the meaning of unfamiliar words
- comprehending explicit and implicit information
- comprehending concrete and abstract information

5

Reading

- classifying and categorizing information
- following a logical or chronological sequence of events

Your listening, speaking and writing skills are not tested by this item type.

Strategies

Before reading

- Skim all the sentences in the text boxes quickly. This will help you understand the topic of the text.

While reading

- Read all the sentences in the text boxes carefully.
- Look for the topic/main sentence. This is probably a general statement about the topic. It will not start with words such as "however" and "nevertheless," nor is it likely to contain pronouns that refer to anything in another sentence.
- Think about the possible relationships between the sentences.

After reading

- Move the topic sentence to the right panel. Do not worry at this stage if you feel unsure. You can re-order sentences later if you change your mind.
- Select a sentence that follows logically from the topic sentence. Repeat this process until you have reconstructed the whole text. Use language clues as well as the meaning of the sentences to do this:

  — Pay attention to grammatical relationships. For example, nouns are often replaced by pronouns in subsequent sentences, and an indefinite article frequently precedes a definite article before the same noun.
  — Look for words and phrases that signal a transition between ideas, for example, "and," "but" or "finally."
  — Pay attention to the sequence of information, such as the chronological order of a narrative or the order of a process.

- Re-read the text after re-ordering the text boxes to check that it makes sense.
- Attempt the item if you are not sure about the correct order. It is better to attempt it than to leave any text boxes unordered.

Practice

Below is a *Re-order paragraphs* item for you to respond to.

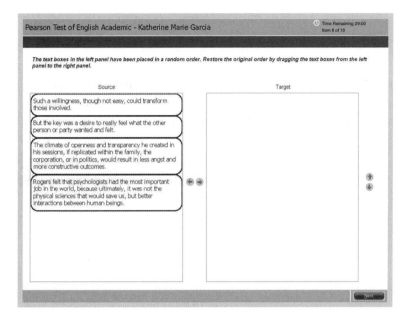

Read the text boxes. Then restore the original order by drawing a line from the text box on the left to the space provided on the right.

Source	Target
Such a willingness, though not easy, could transform those involved.	
But the key was a desire to really feel what the other person or party wanted and felt.	
The climate of openness and transparency he created in his sessions, if replicated within the family, the corporation, or in politics, would result in less angst and more constructive outcomes.	
Rogers felt that psychologists had the most important job in the world, because ultimately, it was not the physical sciences that would save us, but better interactions between human beings.	

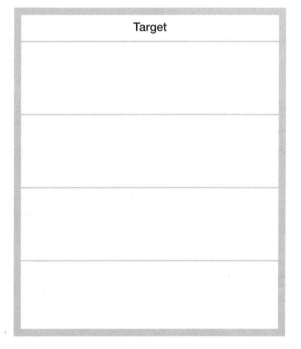

> Remember, during PTE Academic you will give your response by dragging text boxes to the right panel at a test delivery workstation.

Answer key **p.183** **Now check the Answer key.**

Reading: Fill in the blanks

Task

Reading: Fill in the blanks is a reading item type with a single correct answer for each blank. It tests your ability to use context and grammatical cues to identify words that complete a reading text. It assesses reading skills. The image below shows the item type.

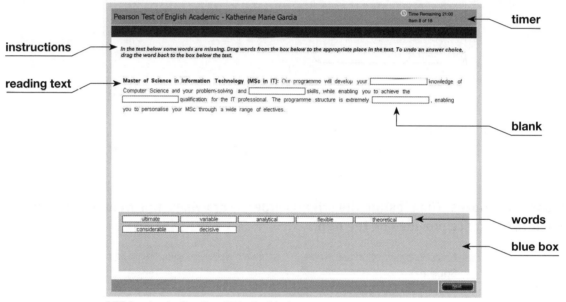

PTE Academic: Reading: Fill in the blanks

Below are the features of *Reading: Fill in the blanks*.

1 Instructions are presented at the top of the computer screen.

> *In the text below some words are missing. Drag words from the box below to the appropriate place in the text. To undo an answer choice, drag the word back to the box below the text.*

2 A reading text with three to five blanks follows.

Master of Science in Information Technology (MSc in IT). Our programme will develop your

[_____] knowledge of Computer Science and your problem-solving and

[_____] skills, while enabling you to achieve the [_____]

qualification for the IT professional. The programme structure is extremely [_____] ,

enabling you to personalise your MSc through a wide range of electives.

3 A blue box with six to eight words follows.

ultimate	variable	analytical	flexible	theoretical
considerable	decisive			

In the box, there are three more words than the number of blanks in the text, so you will not use all the words provided.

To fill a blank, click on a word to select it. Hold the left button of the mouse down and drag the word to the blank where you want to place it. You can also drag words between blanks. If you want to remove a word from a blank, drag the word back to the blue box.

4 Click on the "Next" button to go to the next item. The timer for the reading part will continue running.

The reading texts for this item type are up to 80 words in length. There are four to five *Reading: Fill in the blanks* items in the reading part of PTE Academic, depending on the combination of items in a given test. They are presented together in a single block.

Scoring

If all blanks are filled correctly, you receive the maximum score points for this item type. If one or more blanks are filled incorrectly, partial credit scoring applies. This item type affects the scoring of the following:

Overall score			✔
Communicative skills			
Listening		Speaking	
Reading	✔	Writing	
Enabling skills			
Grammar		Spelling	
Oral fluency		Vocabulary	
Pronunciation		Written discourse	

5

Reading

Reading skills

Reading: Fill in the blanks tests your reading skills in an academic environment. Below are the key skills tested:

- identifying the topic, theme or main ideas
- identifying words and phrases appropriate to the context
- understanding academic vocabulary
- understanding the difference between connotation and denotation
- inferring the meaning of unfamiliar words
- comprehending explicit and implicit information
- comprehending concrete and abstract information
- following a logical or chronological sequence of events

Your listening, speaking and writing skills are not tested by this item type.

Strategies

Before reading

- Skim the entire text quickly, ignoring the blanks. This will help you understand the topic.

While reading

- Fill in the blanks one by one. If you feel unsure about any particular blank, skip it. The more blanks you fill in, the easier the remaining ones will be.
- Use language clues as well as word knowledge to fill in the blanks:
  - Pay attention to the grammar of the sentence. For example, if the blank should contain a plural noun, choose a plural noun from the blue box.
  - Pay attention to the pronouns and logical connectors in the text, and choose words that maintain the right relationships.
  - Pay attention to conventional phrasing. Choose words that normally appear before or after the particular words on either side of the blanks.

After reading

- Re-read the text to check that it makes sense.
- Make changes if necessary and re-read the text.
- Attempt the item if you are not sure about certain blanks. It is better to attempt the item than to leave empty blanks.

Practice

Below is a *Reading: Fill in the blanks* item for you to respond to.

Fill in the blanks by writing the words in the spaces.

Science blogs serve a dual purpose. First, they connect scientists to each other, _____ as modern day intellectual salons. Even _____ scientific papers are now beginning to _____ blogs as references. Second, they connect scientists to the general _____, offering a behind-the-scenes _____ at how science progresses.

public	formal	look	view	world
cite	prescribed	serving		

Remember, during PTE Academic you will give your response by dragging words to blanks in the text at a test delivery workstation.

Answer key p.184 **Now check the Answer key.**

Reading

Reading & writing: Fill in the blanks

Task

Reading & writing: Fill in the blanks is a multiple choice reading item type with a single correct answer for each blank. It tests your ability to use contextual and grammatical cues to identify words that complete a reading text. It assesses both reading and writing skills. The image below shows the item type.

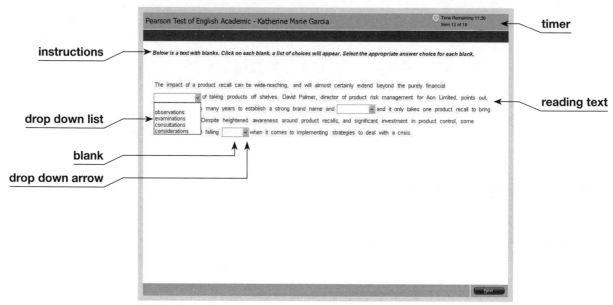

PTE Academic: Reading & writing: Fill in the blanks

Below are the features of *Reading & writing: Fill in the blanks*.

1 Instructions are presented at the top of the computer screen.

> *Below is a text with blanks. Click on each blank, a list of choices will appear. Select the appropriate answer choice for each blank.*

2 A reading text with up to six blanks follows. Each blank has up to five answer choices.

> The impact of a product recall can be wide-reaching, and will almost certainly extend beyond the purely financial [▼] of taking products off shelves. David Palmer, director of product risk management for Aon Limited, points out, "It takes companies many years to establish a strong brand name and [▼] and it only takes one product recall to bring it crashing down." Despite heightened awareness around product recalls, and significant investment in product control, some businesses are still falling [▼] when it comes to implementing strategies to deal with a crisis.

To fill a blank, click on the drop down arrow. This displays a drop down list. To select an answer choice, click on one of the answer choices from the drop down list. To change your choice, click on a different answer.

3 Click on the "Next" button to go to the next item. The timer for the reading part will continue running.

The reading texts for this item type are up to 300 words in length. There are five to six *Reading & writing: Fill in the blanks* items in the reading part of PTE Academic, depending on the combination of items in a given test. They are presented together in a single block.

Scoring

If all blanks are filled correctly, you receive the maximum score points for this item type. If one or more blanks are filled incorrectly, partial credit scoring applies. This item type affects the scoring of the following:

Overall score	✔		
Communicative skills			
Listening		Speaking	
Reading	✔	Writing	✔
Enabling skills			
Grammar		Spelling	
Oral fluency		Vocabulary	
Pronunciation		Written discourse	

Reading and writing skills

Reading & writing: Fill in the blanks is an integrated skills item type that tests both your reading and writing skills in an academic environment. Below are the key skills tested:

Reading

- identifying the topic, theme or main ideas
- identifying words and phrases appropriate to the context
- understanding academic vocabulary
- understanding the difference between connotation and denotation
- inferring the meaning of unfamiliar words
- comprehending explicit and implicit information
- comprehending concrete and abstract information
- following a logical or chronological sequence of events

Writing

- using words and phrases appropriate to the context
- using correct grammar

Your listening and speaking skills are not tested by this item type.

Strategies

Before reading

- Skim the entire text quickly, ignoring the blanks. This will help you understand the topic.

While reading

- Fill in the blanks one by one. If you feel unsure about any particular blank, skip it. The more blanks you fill in, the easier the remaining ones will be.
- Use language clues as well as word knowledge to fill in the blanks:
  — Pay attention to the grammar of the sentence. For example, if the blank should contain a plural noun, choose a plural noun from the drop down list.
  — Pay attention to the pronouns and logical connectors in the text, and choose words that maintain the right relationships.
  — Pay attention to conventional phrasing. Choose words that normally appear before or after the particular words on either side of the blanks.

After reading

- Re-read the text to check that it makes sense.
- Make changes if necessary and re-read the text.
- Attempt an item if you are not sure about certain blanks. It is better to attempt it than to leave empty blanks.

Practice

Below is a *Reading & writing: Fill in the blanks* item for you to respond to.

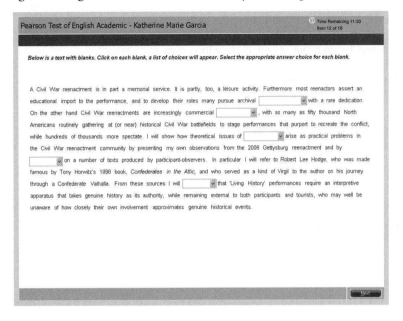

Circle the appropriate answer choice for each blank.

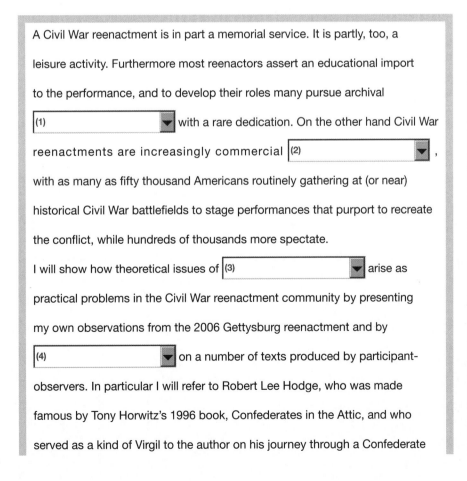

A Civil War reenactment is in part a memorial service. It is partly, too, a leisure activity. Furthermore most reenactors assert an educational import to the performance, and to develop their roles many pursue archival

(1) [_____] with a rare dedication. On the other War reenactments are increasingly commercial (2) [_____], with as many as fifty thousand Americans routinely gathering at (or near) historical Civil War battlefields to stage performances that purport to recreate the conflict, while hundreds of thousands more spectate.

I will show how theoretical issues of (3) [_____] arise as practical problems in the Civil War reenactment community by presenting my own observations from the 2006 Gettysburg reenactment and by

(4) [_____] on a number of texts produced by participant-observers. In particular I will refer to Robert Lee Hodge, who was made famous by Tony Horwitz's 1996 book, Confederates in the Attic, and who served as a kind of Virgil to the author on his journey through a Confederate

(1)
- filing
- research
- searching
- documentation

(2)
- illustrations
- expeditions
- spectacles
- outings

(3)
- authenticity
- pretence
- imitation
- realism

(4)
- leaning
- resting
- counting
- relying

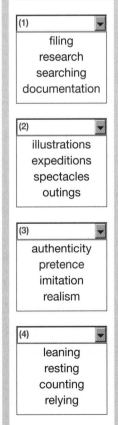

5

Reading

113

Valhalla. From these sources I will (5) [▼] that 'Living History' performances require an interpretive apparatus that takes genuine history as its authority, while remaining external to both participants and tourists, who may well be unaware of how closely their own involvement approximates genuine historical events.

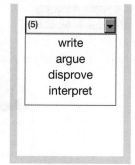

(5) [▼]
write
argue
disprove
interpret

Remember, during PTE Academic you will give your response by clicking on choices at a test delivery workstation.

Answer key p.184 **Now check the Answer key.**

Improving general reading skills

Effective reading

Effective reading, in both everyday and test situations, requires attention to the five areas listed below. Although not all of these areas will be tested in PTE Academic, improving your skills in each area will help your general language proficiency and improve your overall performance in the test.

➤ **Text type**
- Recognize the text type from the context. For example, the presence of an abstract suggests an academic text. The use of formatting identifies genres such as letters, memos or reports. Scene-setting description or dialogue may introduce a story.
- Match your reading style to your purpose for reading and the text type. For example, to understand the key ideas in a news article, you might read the article quickly for the main points. Focus on the title, introduction, opening sentences in paragraphs and the closing sentences at the end. To understand a text in more detail, you may read slowly to identify supporting details. Reading for pleasure can involve reading quickly to follow a storyline without understanding the meaning of every word.

➤ **Topic and gist**
- Focus on the title as it often provides clues about the topic or content of the text. For example, the title "The Hope and Practice of Teaching" indicates that the article is about education.
- Focus on the topic sentences in the paragraphs of a text as they usually provide the main ideas.

➤ **Purpose**
- Refer to the topic and text type to understand the purpose of the text. Text type and topic indicate what the writer intends to do. For example, tell a story, describe an experiment, discuss a problem, or present a lecture.

➤ **Structure and content**
- Pay attention to section headings and sub-headings, paragraphing or main titles to understand the structure of the text.
- Identify basic components in different types of writing to understand the content of the text. For example, in an explanatory text, identify the main ideas, supporting information and conclusions. In a narrative text, recognize the storyline and character-building descriptions.
- Guess the meanings of unfamiliar words and expressions from the context, without constantly referring to a dictionary during the reading process.
- Understand the words and expressions which refer to information elsewhere in the text, such as "this," "in this way," "his," "her." Locate the information in the text. For example, in "Many children were found to have drunk bottled milk when they were infants. This is common behavior in young children," "This" refers to the act of drinking bottled milk.

➤ **Writer's point of view**

- Understand the writer's point of view by referring to the title, the topic sentences, organization of the argument, and concluding statements at the end.
- Identify words and expressions signaling the writer's points of view, feelings or attitudes. For example, "I am uncomfortable with that argument" indicates that the writer has concerns about the argument and probably has a different point of view.

Understanding your strengths and weaknesses

Improving your reading skills starts with an understanding of your own strengths and weaknesses. This will allow you to concentrate on the areas which need to be improved in general, or specifically as preparation for taking PTE Academic. Use the checklist below to assess your current reading skills and to decide on priority areas for improvement.

Effective reading	My current proficiency level			Priority for improvement
	High	Medium	Low	
Text type				
I can recognize text types quickly by scanning a text.				
I can match my reading style to my purpose for reading and the text type to read effectively.				
Topic and gist				
I can use the title to guess the content of the text.				
I can use the topic sentences to understand the main ideas of the text.				
Purpose				
I can understand the purpose of the text by referring to the topic and text type.				
Structure and content				
I can understand the structure of the text by paying attention to section headings and sub-headings, paragraphing or main titles.				
I can understand the content of the text by identifying basic components in different types of writing.				
I can guess the meaning of unfamiliar words from the context without checking a dictionary.				
I can locate and understand the words or expressions that refer to other information in the text.				

Effective reading	My current proficiency level			Priority for improvement
	High	Medium	Low	
Writer's point of view				
I can understand the writer's point of view by referring to the title, the topic sentences, organization of the argument, and concluding statements at the end.				
I can identify words and expressions signaling the writer's point of view, feelings or attitude.				

Developing your reading skills

Follow the suggestions below to improve your general reading skills:

➤ **Read more. Take every opportunity to read.**
  - Read for pleasure. Choose topics that you enjoy and materials that are not too difficult.
  - Develop a habit of reading in English every day.

➤ **Practice reading.**
  - Read tables of content, chapter headings or summaries to get an overall idea of the book or text. Select chapters or parts of chapters for intensive reading for meaning.
  - Read lecture notes or presentation materials to understand the main points and identify linking expressions such as "However, the most important factor" or "The next section elaborates …."
  - Try to answer comprehension questions for reading passages in online English language courses and textbooks. Use the answer keys provided to check your answers.
  - Take an online or classroom-based reading course. This will allow you to get reading practice that is tailored to your proficiency level and needs.

➤ **Build your vocabulary.**
  - Note words or expressions that you find useful during the reading process, and look up their meanings in a dictionary when necessary.
  - Develop a habit of noting definitions of words from the dictionary, including different parts of speech when necessary. For example, make a note of the difference between "diverge" and "divergence," or "critic" and "critical."
  - Use a thesaurus to find synonyms for familiar or unfamiliar words that you read. This will increase your range of expression. Check synonyms in a dictionary to understand their exact meanings.
  - Expand and consolidate your knowledge of the words used frequently in academic texts. You may refer to *Longman Exams Dictionary* for a list of academic words as well as lists of the most frequent words categorized by topic.

5

Reading

Reading strategies

➤ **Read for pleasure.**

- Do not interrupt your reading to look up words in a dictionary. Note unfamiliar words if you wish to check them later. Guess the meanings of words from the context, or simply carry on reading. Remember that even native speakers of English do not understand every word they read.

- Do not continue any reading material you are not enjoying. Change what you are reading.

- Build your reading fluency. Read fast so that you can follow the reading material in general. A general guideline for fast reading is to move your eyes over the text so quickly that you cannot comfortably pronounce the words as you read.

➤ **Read for information.**

- Read the text quickly to determine the type of text and to find the title, section headings, table of contents or abstract. These provide clues to the content and structure of the text.

- Read through the first two or three paragraphs to get a better idea of the topic and to discover the writer's point of view.

- Read for main points and items of interest. Note the way in which the discussion or argument is developed. For example, is there a main point followed by examples? Are there arguments for or against a proposal? Does the writer use a past, present, or future time frame?

➤ **Respond to comprehension questions.**

- Read the text quickly first, as described above in "Read for information."

- Read the questions quickly to get an idea of what you are required to look for. Some questions may ask for specific information, identification of the gist, or attitudes and points of view. Some questions may ask for understanding of what a word or expression refers to elsewhere in the text. For example, "What does 'this' in line 12 refer to?" Some questions may ask for the meanings of words and expressions in the text.

- Read each question again carefully to ensure that you understand what is being asked. Then skim the text to find the answer.

Sources of reading material

- The Internet includes examples of a wide variety of reading material.

- News articles, essays and reports provide good examples of organization. They often put the main point at the beginning, use topic sentences to start paragraphs and develop an argument or discussion in a logical way. As these genres generally cover a range of topics, they are good sources of vocabulary and expressions in specific subject areas. They can also provide useful examples of logical argument and the use of linking words and phrases to express relationships between ideas.

- Online English courses and textbooks provide material on topics related to different fields of study or personal interests.

- Academic journals in different fields of study contain articles with abstracts which summarize purpose, content and conclusions.
- Novels and short stories are useful to enhance the pleasure of reading, and to build understanding of the expression of ideas and feelings.

Preparing for PTE Academic

To prepare for PTE Academic, you should practice the reading skills that you will be assessed on in the test.

- Read Chapter 5 of the *Official Guide* to obtain information on all aspects of the reading item types in the test and practice responding to the example items.
- Use the CD-ROM included with the *Official Guide* to gain further practice in responding to reading items.
- Use the PTE Academic Tutorial available at www.pearsonpte.com to learn how to respond to these items in the actual test.
- Take a practice test available at www.pearsonpte.com.

Refer to the section "Resources" in Chapter 2 of the *Official Guide* for further information.

5

Reading

PTE Academic

Listening

Part 3: Listening of PTE Academic tests your ability to understand spoken English in an academic environment. It also tests your ability to understand a variety of accents, both native and non-native.

Listening skills

The listening skills tested in PTE Academic include the following:

- identifying the topic, theme or main ideas
- summarizing the main idea
- identifying supporting points or examples
- understanding academic vocabulary
- inferring the meaning of unfamiliar words
- identifying words and phrases appropriate to the context
- comprehending explicit and implicit information
- comprehending concrete and abstract information
- classifying and categorizing information
- following an oral sequencing of information
- forming a conclusion from what a speaker says
- predicting how a speaker may continue
- identifying errors in a transcription
- identifying a speaker's purpose, style, tone or attitude
- inferring the context, purpose or tone
- comprehending variations in tone, speed, accent

- identifying specific details, facts, opinions and definitions or sequences of events
- identifying the overall organization of information and connections between pieces of information
- evaluating and synthesizing information
- summarizing the main idea

Overview

General listening instructions are presented before Part 3: Listening.

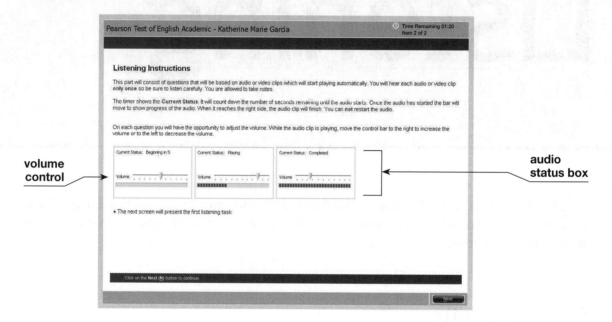

The audio status box on screen shows how long until the audio or video recording starts and the progress of the recording while you are listening and/or watching. You can adjust the volume by moving the slider on the volume control. You must listen to all the audio and cannot move on to the next item until the audio has finished playing.

Listening item types require you to understand an audio or video recording of an authentic lecture, presentation or dialogue from an academic source.

Eight item types appear in the listening part of PTE Academic. The total time to complete the listening part of the test is approximately 45–57 minutes, depending on the combination of items in a given test. Some of the item types are integrated and assess both listening as well as reading and writing skills.

Part 3 (listening) total time: 45–57 minutes

Item type	Task	Skills assessed	Recording length
Summarize spoken text	After listening to a recording, write a summary of 50–70 words.	listening and writing	60–90 seconds
Multiple-choice, choose multiple answers	After listening to a recording, answer a multiple-choice question on the content or tone of the recording by selecting more than one response.	listening	40–90 seconds
Fill in the blanks	The transcription of a recording appears on screen with several blanks. While listening to the recording, type the missing words into the blanks.	listening and writing	30–60 seconds
Highlight correct summary	After listening to a recording, select the paragraph that best summarizes the recording.	listening and reading	30–90 seconds
Multiple-choice, choose single answer	After listening to a recording, answer a multiple-choice question on the content or tone of the recording by selecting one response.	listening	30–60 seconds
Select missing word	After listening to a recording, select the missing word or group of words that completes the recording.	listening	20–70 seconds
Highlight incorrect words	The transcription of a recording appears on screen. While listening to the recording, identify the words in the transcription that differ from what is said.	listening and reading	15–50 seconds
Write from dictation	After listening to a recording of a sentence, type the sentence.	listening and writing	3–5 seconds

The recordings focus on academic subjects in the humanities, natural sciences or social sciences. They contain characteristics of actual speech, such as accents and dialects, fillers, hesitations, false starts, self corrections and variations in delivery speed. Although you may not be familiar with the topics presented, all the information you need to answer the items is contained in the recordings.

Each recording is played only once. You may take notes using the Erasable Noteboard Booklet and pen, and use these notes as a guide when answering the items.

With the exception of *Summarize spoken text*, listening item types are not timed individually. You can refer to the timer in the upper right-hand corner of the computer screen, "Time Remaining," which counts down the amount of time remaining for the listening part.

6

Listening

Summarize spoken text

333333 Task

Summarize spoken text is an item type that tests your ability to comprehend, analyze and combine information from a lecture, and then summarize the key points in writing. It assesses both listening and writing skills. The image below shows the item type.

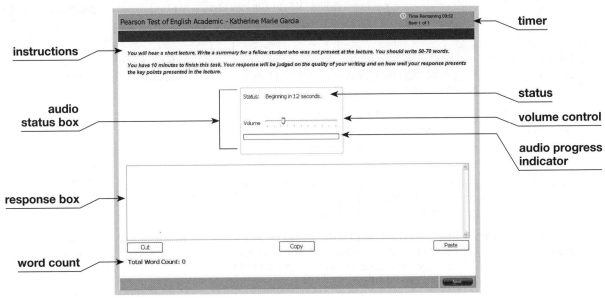

PTE Academic: Summarize spoken text

Below are the features of *Summarize spoken text*.

1 Instructions are presented at the top of the computer screen.

> *You will hear a short lecture. Write a summary for a fellow student who was not present at the lecture. You should write 50–70 words.*
>
> *You will have 10 minutes to finish this task. Your response will be judged on the quality of your writing and on how well your response presents the key points presented in the lecture.*

2 In the audio status box, the status will count down from 12 seconds. Then a recording will play automatically.

124

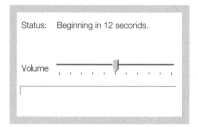

The audio progress indicator represents the entire duration of the lecture. So if the lecture is short, the bar moves faster. If the lecture is long, the bar moves slower.

The status will change to "Playing." To adjust the volume of the recording, move the slider left to decrease and right to increase. You can adjust the volume at any time while the recording is playing. The audio progress indicator features a blue bar that will gradually move to the right as the recording continues. When the recording finishes, the status will change to "Completed."

3 A response box follows.

Use this space to type your summary. You can select text within the response box with the mouse, and use the "Cut," "Copy" and "Paste" buttons to edit your response. The "Total Word Count" keeps track of the number of words written and updates as you type.

 **Play the CD to listen to the recording that goes with this item.**

4 The timer will count down from 10 minutes for this item type. Click on the "Next" button to go to the next item.

The recordings for this item type run for approximately 60–90 seconds. Each recording will play only once. There are two to three *Summarize spoken text* items in PTE Academic, depending on the combination of items in a given test. They are presented together in a single block. This item type is individually timed. You have 10 minutes to answer each item of this type. After 10 minutes, the test will automatically move on to the next item.

Scoring

Your response for *Summarize spoken text* is judged on the quality of your writing and on how well your response presents the key points in the lecture. Your score is based on five factors:

➤ **Content:** Does your response summarize the main points in the lecture?

Content is scored by determining if all the key points of the lecture have been addressed without misrepresenting the purpose or topic. If your summary misinterprets the topic or the purpose of the lecture, you will not receive any score points for your summary on any of the five factors. Your summary will be scored zero. The best responses clearly summarize the main points and condense essential supporting points. They focus on the topic, including only key information and essential supporting points.

➤ **Form:** Does your response meet the length requirement of between 50 and 70 words?

Form is scored by counting the number of words in your response. You will receive full credit if your response is between 50 and 70 words. Writing less than 50 words or more than 70 words will decrease your score. If your summary contains less than 40 words or more than 100 words, you will not receive any score points for your summary on any of the five factors. Your summary will be scored zero.

➤ **Grammar:** Does your response demonstrate correct grammatical usage?

Grammar is scored by determining if the basic structure of the sentences is correct. The best responses use concise sentences that clearly communicate the intended meaning.

➤ **Vocabulary:** Does your response demonstrate correct and appropriate word choice and usage?

Vocabulary is scored according to its relevance to the lecture and its appropriateness in an academic environment. The appropriate use of synonyms is also scored. The best responses use words from the lecture appropriately, demonstrate an understanding of the context and use synonyms effectively to show variety in language use.

➤ **Spelling:** Does your response demonstrate correct and consistent use of a single spelling convention?

PTE Academic recognizes English spelling conventions from the United States, the United Kingdom, Australia and Canada. However, one spelling convention should be used consistently in a given response.

Partial credit scoring applies to *Summarize spoken text.* No credit is given for no response or an irrelevant response. This item type affects the scoring of the following:

Overall score			✔
Communicative skills			
Listening	✔	Speaking	
Reading		Writing	✔
Enabling skills			
Grammar	✔	Spelling	✔
Oral fluency		Vocabulary	✔
Pronunciation		Written discourse	

Listening and writing skills

Summarize spoken text is an integrated skills item type that tests both your listening and writing skills in an academic environment. Below are the key skills tested:

Listening

- identifying the topic, theme or main ideas
- summarizing the main idea
- identifying supporting points or examples
- identifying a speaker's purpose, style, tone or attitude
- understanding academic vocabulary
- inferring the meaning of unfamiliar words
- comprehending explicit and implicit information
- comprehending concrete and abstract information
- classifying and categorizing information
- following an oral sequencing of information
- comprehending variations in tone, speed, accent

Writing

- writing a summary
- writing under timed conditions
- taking notes while listening to a recording
- communicating the main points of a lecture in writing
- organizing sentences and paragraphs in a logical way
- using words and phrases appropriate to the context
- using correct grammar
- using correct spelling
- using correct mechanics

Your speaking skills are not tested by this item type, and your reading skills are only used to read the instructions.

Strategies

While listening

- Pay attention to the content of the lecture. It is important that you understand what you hear because you will have to summarize the lecture in your own words.
- Take notes using the Erasable Noteboard Booklet and pen. Focus on key words. Do not attempt to take notes word-for-word. You may miss important information if you try to write too much.
- Review your notes and plan your summary when the recording stops.

6

Listening

While writing

- Summarize the lecture in your own words. Refer to your notes when necessary.
- Use an overview sentence to introduce the summary.
- Include all of the main ideas from the lecture and provide some supporting details.
- Use grammatical structures that you feel confident about.

After writing

- Check the content of your summary. Does it contain all of the key information?
- Check the total word count. Does it fall between 50 and 70 words? If not, adjust the text length accordingly.
- Check grammar, spelling and punctuation, and make corrections where necessary.

Practice

Below is a *Summarize spoken text* item for you to respond to.

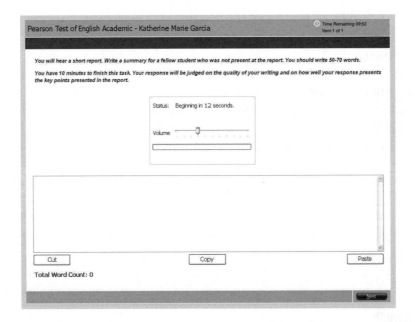

Listen to the lecture only once. Then write your summary in the space provided on the next page. To simulate the test conditions, give yourself only 10 minutes to respond to this item.

> Remember, during PTE Academic you will type in your response at a test delivery workstation.

....

....

....

....

....

....

....

....

....

....

....

....

Answer key   p.185   **Now check the Answer key.**

Multiple-choice, choose multiple answers

Task

Multiple-choice, choose multiple answers is a multiple-choice listening item type with more than one correct response. It tests your ability to analyze, interpret and evaluate a brief audio or video recording on an academic subject. It assesses listening skills. The image below shows the item type.

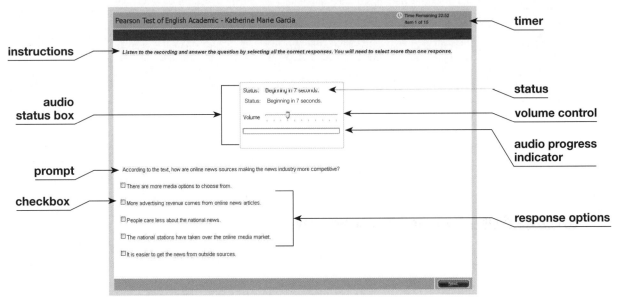

PTE Academic: Multiple-choice, choose multiple answers

Below are the features of *Multiple-choice, choose multiple answers*.

1 Instructions are presented at the top of the computer screen.

> *Listen to the recording and answer the question by selecting all the correct responses. You will need to select more than one response.*

2 In the audio status box, the status will count down from seven seconds. Then a recording will play automatically.

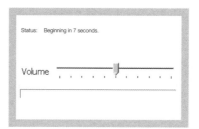

> Status: Beginning in 7 seconds.
>
> Volume

The audio progress indicator represents the entire duration of the recording. So if the recording is short, the bar moves faster. If the recording is long, the bar moves slower.

The status will change to "Playing." To adjust the volume of the recording, move the slider left to decrease and right to increase. You can adjust the volume at any time while the recording is playing. The audio progress indicator features a blue bar that will gradually move to the right as the recording continues. When the recording finishes, the status will change to "Completed."

3 A prompt with five to seven response options follows.

> According to the speaker, how are online news sources making the news industry more competitive?
>
> ☐ There are more media options to choose from.
>
> ☐ More advertising revenue comes from online news articles.
>
> ☐ People care less about the national news.
>
> ☐ The national stations have taken over the online media market.
>
> ☐ It is easier to get the news from outside sources.

To select a response, click on the corresponding checkbox or the response itself. Your response will be highlighted in yellow. To deselect your response, click on the checkbox or the response again. To change your responses, click on a different checkbox or a different response.

10 **Play the CD to listen to the recording that goes with this item.**

4 Click on the "Next" button to go to the next item. The timer for the listening part will continue running.

The recordings for this item type run for approximately 40–90 seconds. Each recording will play only once. There are two to three *Multiple-choice, choose multiple answers* items in the listening part of PTE Academic, depending on the combination of items in a given test. They are presented together in a single block.

6

Listening

131

Scoring

If all response options are correct, you receive the maximum score points for this item type. If one or more response options are incorrect, partial credit scoring applies. This item type affects the scoring of the following:

Overall score		✔
Communicative skills		
Listening	✔	Speaking
Reading		Writing
Enabling skills		
Grammar		Spelling
Oral fuency		Vocabulary
Pronunciation		Written discourse

Listening skills

Multiple-choice, choose multiple answers tests your listening skills in an academic environment. Any of the following listening skills could be tested by this item type:

➤ **Main idea or gist:** Listen for and identify the main idea or theme of the recording. For example, "What aspects of commercial airline travel does the speaker discuss?"

➤ **Detailed information:** Listen for and identify specific details, facts, opinions, definitions or sequences of events. For example, "According to the speaker what are the benefits of flexitime?"

➤ **Speaker's purpose:** Listen for and understand the function of what the speaker says, or identify the reasons why the speaker mentions specific pieces of information. For example, "Why does the speaker say 'music is language'?"

➤ **Organization:** Listen for and identify the overall organization and connections between pieces of information. This evaluates your ability to link different parts of the recording together. For example, "How does the speaker link the opening to the main argument of the lecture?"

➤ **Inference:** Listen for information that helps you infer meanings, form generalizations, make predictions, find relationships or draw conclusions. For example, "What can be inferred about the role of small businesses in the United States described by the speaker?"

➤ **Stylistics:** Listen for and identify the speaker's attitude, feelings or degree of certainty on an issue. For example, "What are the speaker's attitudes towards electronic surveillance systems?"

Your speaking and writing skills are not tested by this item type, and your reading skills are only used to read the instructions, prompt and response options.

Strategies

Before listening

- Read the prompt carefully. This will help you understand what to listen for.
- Skim the response options quickly.

While listening

- Take notes using the Erasable Noteboard Booklet and pen if you want to. Focus on key words. Do not attempt to take notes word-for-word. You may miss important information if you try to write too much.
- Continue listening until the end of the recording, even if you think you have already heard the information you need. Sometimes speakers revise what they have said, or add extra information.

After listening

- Re-read the prompt.
- Read the response options and select the correct ones.

    — First eliminate any response options which you feel sure are incorrect.
    — Then eliminate response options containing information that is not mentioned.
    — Do not select an option just because it contains words from the recording. Sometimes incorrect options contain the same words from the recording.

- Do not change your first responses unless you feel sure that they are incorrect.

Practice

Below is a *Multiple-choice, choose multiple answers* item for you to respond to.

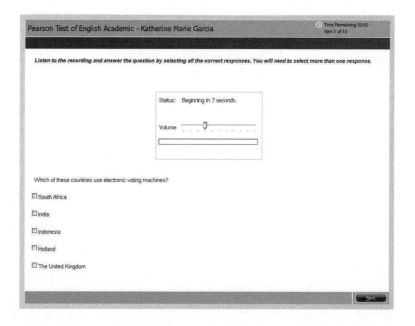

11 Read the prompt. Then listen to the recording only once and select all the correct responses.

Which of these countries use electronic voting machines?

- ☐ South Africa

- ☐ India

- ☐ Indonesia

- ☐ Holland

- ☐ the United Kingdom

Remember, during PTE Academic you will give your response by clicking on responses at a test delivery workstation.

Answer key | **p.186** | Now check the Answer key.

Fill in the blanks

Task

Fill in the blanks is an item type that tests your ability to listen for missing words in a recording and type the missing words into a transcription. It assesses both listening and writing skills. The image below shows the item type.

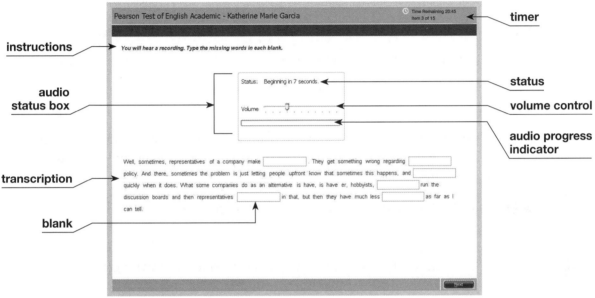

PTE Academic: Fill in the blanks

Below are the features of *Fill in the blanks*.

1 Instructions are presented at the top of the computer screen.

> *You will hear a recording. Type the missing words in each blank.*

2 In the audio status box, the status will count down from seven seconds. Then a recording will play automatically.

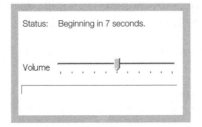

> The audio progress indicator represents the entire duration of the recording. So if the recording is short, the bar moves faster. If the recording is long, the bar moves slower.

The status will change to "Playing." To adjust the volume of the recording, move the slider left to decrease and right to increase. You can adjust the volume at any time while the recording is playing. The audio progress indicator features a blue bar that will gradually move to the right as the recording continues. When the recording finishes, the status will change to "Completed."

3 A transcription of the recording with up to seven blanks follows.

Well, sometimes, representatives of a company make misstatements. They get something wrong

regarding [   ] policy. And there, sometimes the problem is just letting people

upfront know that sometimes this happens, and [   ] quickly when it does.

What some companies do as an alternative is have ... [   ], aficionados run

the discussion boards and then representatives participate in that, but then they have much less

[   ] as far as I can tell.

To respond, type the missing words into the blanks. To change your response, select your original response and then retype it. You can also use the "Tab" key on your keyboard to move the cursor between the blanks.

 **Play the CD to listen to the recording that goes with this item.**

4 Click on the "Next" button to go to the next item. The timer for the listening part will continue running.

The recordings for this item type run for approximately 30–60 seconds. Each recording will play only once. There are two to three *Fill in the blanks* items in the listening part of PTE Academic, depending on the combination of items in a given test. They are presented together in a single block.

Scoring

Your score on *Fill in the blanks* is based on the following factor:

➤ **Content:** Does your response include all the missing words?

Content is scored by counting the number of right words with correct spelling in your response. Each correct word spelled correctly scores 1 point.

If all blanks are filled with the right word spelled correctly, you receive the maximum score points for this item type. If one or more blanks are filled incorrectly, partial credit scoring applies. This item type affects the scoring of the following:

Overall score			✔
Communicative skills			
Listening	✔	Speaking	
Reading		Writing	✔
Enabling skills			
Grammar		Spelling	
Oral fluency		Vocabulary	
Pronunciation		Written discourse	

Listening and writing skills

Fill in the blanks is an integrated skills item type that tests both your listening and writing skills in an academic environment. Below are the key skills tested:

Listening

- identifying words and phrases appropriate to the context
- understanding academic vocabulary
- comprehending explicit and implicit information
- following an oral sequencing of information

Writing

- writing from dictation
- using words and phrases appropriate to the context
- using correct grammar
- using correct spelling

Your speaking skills are not tested by this item type, and your reading skills are only used to read the instructions and the transcription.

Strategies

Before listening

- Skim the text quickly. This will help you understand what you hear.
- Place the cursor in the first blank so that you are prepared to type.

6

Listening

While listening

- Follow the written text as you hear it spoken.
- Take notes using the Erasable Noteboard Booklet and pen if you want to, and fill in the blanks after listening.
- Type a word in the first blank. Do not stop to re-read what you have typed.
- Move the cursor to the next blank so you are prepared to type.
- Continue filling in the blanks until the recording stops.

After listening

- Check your responses and correct them if necessary.

  — Do the completed sentences make sense?
  — Do the words you have typed fit the sentences grammatically?
  — Are the spellings of the words you have typed correct?

- Make changes only if you are sure that the words you typed are incorrect.

Practice

Below is a *Fill in the blanks* item for you to respond to.

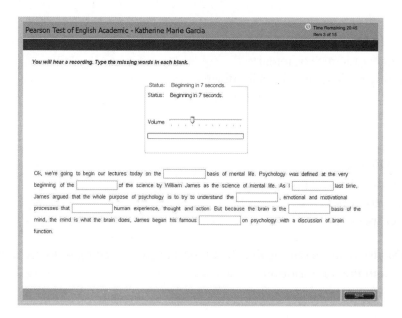

13 **Listen to the recording only once. As you listen, write the missing words in the blanks of the transcription.**

OK, we're going to begin our lectures today on the [_____] basis of mental life.

Psychology was defined at the very beginning of the [_____] of the science by

William James as the science of mental life. As I [_____] last time, James argued

that the whole purpose of psychology is to try to understand the [_____], emotional

and motivational processes that [_____] human experience, thought and action. But

because the brain is the [_____] basis of the mind, the mind is what the brain does,

James began his famous [_____] on psychology with a discussion of brain function.

Remember, during PTE Academic you will give your response by typing words into blanks at a test delivery workstation.

Answer key p.188   **Now check the Answer key.**

Highlight correct summary

Task

Highlight correct summary is an item type that tests your ability to comprehend, analyze and combine information from a recording and identify the most accurate summary of the recording. It assesses both listening and reading skills. The image below shows the item type.

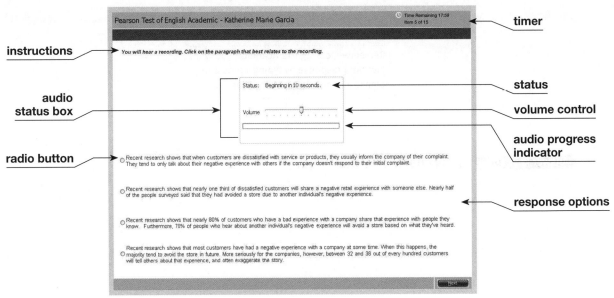

PTE Academic: Highlight correct summary

Below are the features of *Highlight correct summary*.

1 Instructions are presented at the top of the computer screen.

> *You will hear a recording. Click on the paragraph that best relates to the recording.*

2 In the audio status box, the status will count down from 10 seconds. Then a recording will play automatically.

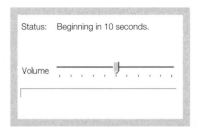

Status: Beginning in 10 seconds.

Volume

The audio progress indicator represents the entire duration of the recording. So if the recording is short, the bar moves faster. If the recording is long, the bar moves slower.

The status will change to "Playing." To adjust the volume of the recording, move the slider left to decrease and right to increase. You can adjust the volume at any time while the recording is playing. The audio progress indicator features a blue bar that will gradually move to the right as the recording continues. When the recording finishes, the status will change to "Completed."

3 Three to five paragraphs follow.

○ Recent research shows that when customers are dissatisfied with service or products, they usually inform the company of their complaint. They tend to only talk about their negative experience with others if the company doesn't respond to their initial complaint.

○ Recent research shows that nearly one third of dissatisfied customers will share a negative retail experience with someone else. Nearly half of the people surveyed said that they had avoided a store due to another individual's negative experience.

○ Recent research shows that nearly 80% of customers who had a bad experience with a company will share that experience with people they know. Furthermore, 70% of people who hear about another individual's negative experience will avoid a store based on what they've heard.

○ Recent research shows that most customers have had a negative experience with a company at some time. When this happens, the majority tend to avoid the store in future. More seriously for the companies, however, between 32 and 36 out of every hundred customers will tell others about that experience, and exaggerate the story.

To select a paragraph, click on the corresponding radio button or the paragraph itself. Your response will be highlighted in yellow. To deselect your response, click on the radio button or the paragraph again. To change your response, click on a different radio button or a different paragraph.

 Play the CD to listen to the recording that goes with this item.

4 Click on the "Next" button to go to the next item. The timer for the listening part will continue running.

The recordings for this item type run for approximately 30–90 seconds. Each recording will play only once. The paragraphs for this item type are up to 60 words in length. There are two to three *Highlight correct summary* items in PTE Academic, depending on the combination of items in a given test. They are presented together in a single block.

Scoring

Your response is scored as either correct or incorrect. No credit is given for no response or an incorrect response. This item type affects the scoring of the following:

Overall score		✔
Communicative skills		
Listening	✔	Speaking
Reading	✔	Writing
Enabling skills		
Grammar		Spelling
Oral fluency		Vocabulary
Pronunciation		Written discourse

Listening and reading skills

Highlight correct summary is an integrated skills item type that tests both your listening and reading skills in an academic environment. Below are the key skills tested:

Listening

- identifying the topic, theme or main ideas
- identifying supporting points or examples
- understanding academic vocabulary
- inferring the meaning of unfamiliar words
- comprehending explicit and implicit information
- comprehending concrete and abstract information
- classifying and categorizing information
- following an oral sequencing of information
- comprehending variations in tone, speed, accent

Reading

- identifying supporting points or examples
- identifying the most accurate summary
- understanding academic vocabulary
- inferring the meaning of unfamiliar words
- comprehending concrete and abstract information
- classifying and categorizing information
- following a logical or chronological sequence of events
- evaluating the quality and usefulness of texts

Your speaking and writing skills are not tested by this item type.

Strategies

Before listening

- Watch the status in the audio status box and be prepared to focus on listening when the recording begins.
- Skim the response options quickly.

While listening

- Concentrate on what you hear. Do not read the paragraphs.
- Take notes using the Erasable Noteboard Booklet and pen if you want to. Focus on key words. Do not attempt to take notes word-for-word. You may miss important information if you try to write too much.

After listening

- Read the paragraphs carefully. Choose the one that best summarizes the recording.
    — First eliminate the paragraphs containing incorrect information.
    — Then eliminate the paragraphs containing information which is not mentioned in the recording.
    — Eliminate the paragraphs which contain details, but omit the main points.
- Attempt the item if you are not sure which is the correct paragraph. It is better to attempt the item than to leave it unanswered.

Practice

Below is a *Highlight correct summary* item for you to respond to.

15 **Listen to the recording only once. Then select the paragraph that best relates to the recording.**

○ The speaker explains the difference between electrochemistry and chemical metallurgy. The similarities and differences between the two are discussed, as well as factors that determine the differences.

○ The speaker explains the class objective and procedures to students. He also tells the class his background information and that they have the choice of attending a class either at 8 AM or 9 AM.

○ The speaker gives his personal background related to the subject matter of the course. He discusses his background in education as well as research, and his experience teaching at this university.

○ The speaker tells about his experience at the University of Toronto and his PhD studies in electrochemistry there. He explains why he stayed in Canada for a longer period of time than the two years that he had planned.

Remember, during PTE Academic you will give your response by clicking on a response at a test delivery workstation.

Answer key **p.188** **Now check the Answer key.**

Multiple-choice, choose single answer

Task

Multiple-choice, choose single answer is a multiple-choice listening item type with a single correct response. It tests your ability to analyze, interpret and evaluate a brief recording on an academic subject. It assesses listening skills. The image below shows the item type.

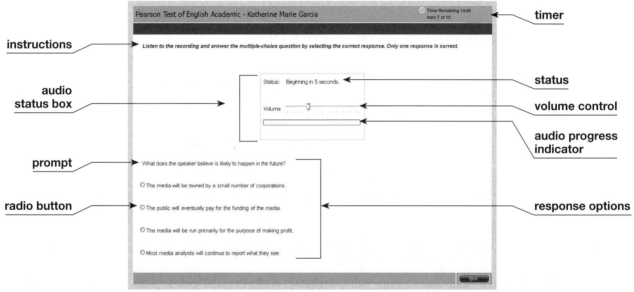

PTE Academic: Multiple-choice, choose single answer

Below are the features of *Multiple-choice, choose single answer*.

1 Instructions are presented at the top of the computer screen.

> *Listen to the recording and answer the multiple-choice question by selecting the correct response. Only one response is correct.*

2 In the audio status box, the status will count down from five seconds. Then a recording will play automatically.

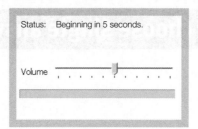

The audio progress indicator represents the entire duration of the recording. So if the recording is short, the bar moves faster. If the recording is long, the bar moves slower.

The status will change to "Playing." To adjust the volume of the recording, move the slider left to decrease and right to increase. You can adjust the volume at any time while the recording is playing. The audio progress indicator features a blue bar that will gradually move to the right as the recording continues. When the recording finishes, the status will change to "Completed."

3 A prompt with three to five response options follows.

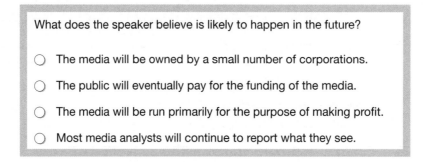

To select a response, click on the corresponding radio button or the response itself. Your response will be highlighted in yellow. To deselect your response, click on the radio button or the response again. To change your response, click on a different radio button or a different response.

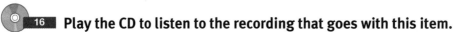 **Play the CD to listen to the recording that goes with this item.**

4 Click on the "Next" button to go to the next item. The timer for the listening part will continue running.

The recordings for this item type run for approximately 30–60 seconds. Each recording will play only once. There are two to three *Multiple-choice, choose single answer* items in the listening part of PTE Academic, depending on the combination of items in a given test. They are presented together in a single block.

Scoring

Your response is scored as either correct or incorrect. No credit is given for no response or an incorrect response. This item type affects the scoring of the following:

Overall score		✔
Communicative skills		
Listening	✔	Speaking
Reading		Writing
Enabling skills		
Grammar		Spelling
Oral fluency		Vocabulary
Pronunciation		Written discourse

Listening skills

Multiple-choice, choose single answer tests your listening skills in an academic environment. Any of the following listening skills could be tested by this item type:

➤ **Main idea or gist:** Listen for and identify the main idea or theme of the recording. For example, "Which of the following statements is the best summary of the speaker's main point?"

➤ **Detailed information:** Listen for and identify specific details, facts, opinions, definitions or sequences of events. For example, "According to the speaker what is the main benefit of nuclear energy?"

➤ **Speaker's purpose:** Listen for and understand the function of what the speaker says, or identify the reasons why the speaker mentions specific pieces of information. For example, "Why does the speaker say 'globalization is nothing new'?"

➤ **Organization:** Listen for and identify the overall organization and connections between pieces of information. This evaluates your ability to link different parts of the recording together. For example, "How does the speaker link the opening to the main argument of the lecture?"

➤ **Inference:** Listen for information that helps you infer meanings, form generalizations, make predictions, find relationships or draw conclusions. For example, "What can be inferred about early childhood education described by the speaker?"

➤ **Stylistics:** Listen for and identify the speaker's attitude, feelings or degree of certainty on an issue. For example, "What is the speaker's attitude towards Tupper's project?"

Your speaking and writing skills are not tested with this item type, and your reading skills are only used to read the instructions, prompt, and response options.

6

Listening

Strategies

Before listening

- Read the prompt carefully. This will help you understand what to listen for.
- Skim the response options quickly.

While listening

- Take notes using the Erasable Noteboard Booklet and pen if you want to. Focus on key words. Do not attempt to take notes word-for-word. You may miss important information if you try to write too much.
- Continue listening until the end of the recording, even if you think you have already heard the information you need. Sometimes speakers revise what they have said, or add extra information.

After listening

- Re-read the prompt.
- Read the response options and select the correct one.

  — First eliminate any response options which you feel sure are incorrect.
  — Then eliminate the response options containing information which is not mentioned.
  — Do not select an option just because it contains words from the recording. Sometimes incorrect options contain the same words from the recording.

- Do not change your first response unless you feel sure that it is incorrect.
- Attempt the item if you are not sure which is the correct response. It is better to attempt the item than to leave it unanswered.

Practice

Below is a *Multiple-choice, choose single answer* item for you to respond to.

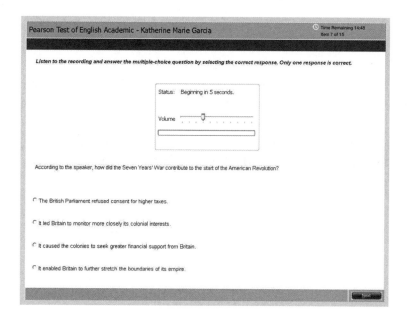

 17 **Read the prompt. Then listen to the recording only once and select the correct response.**

According to the speaker, how did the Seven Years' War contribute to the start of the American Revolution?

○ The British Parliament refused consent for higher taxes.

○ It led Britain to monitor more closely its colonial interests.

○ It caused the colonies to seek greater financial support from Britain.

○ It enabled Britain to further stretch the boundaries of its empire.

Remember, during PTE Academic you will give your response by clicking on a response at a test delivery workstation.

Answer key p.190 **Now check the Answer key.**

6

Listening

Select missing word

Task

Select missing word is an item type that tests your ability to predict what a speaker will say based on contextual clues in a recording. It assesses listening skills. The image below shows the item type.

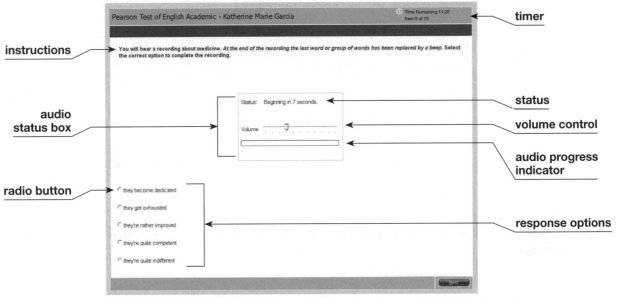

PTE Academic: Select missing word

Below are the features of *Select missing word*.

1 Instructions are presented at the top of the computer screen.

> You will hear a recording about medicine. *At the end of the recording the last word or group of words has been replaced by a beep.* Select the correct option to complete the recording.

The topic of the recording will vary by item. The topic will be stated in the instructions.

> While the topic may vary, the task will always be the same.

2 In the audio status box, the status will count down from seven seconds. Then a recording will play automatically.

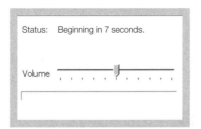

The audio progress indicator represents the entire duration of the recording. So if the recording is short, the bar moves faster. If the recording is long, the bar moves slower.

The status will change to "Playing." To adjust the volume of the recording, move the slider left to decrease and right to increase. You can adjust the volume at any time while the recording is playing. The audio progress indicator features a blue bar that will gradually move to the right as the recording continues. When the recording finishes, the status will change to "Completed."

The last word or group of words in the recording is replaced by a beep.

3 Three to five response options follow.

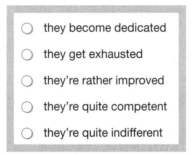

To select a response, click on the corresponding radio button or the response itself. Your response will be highlighted in yellow. To deselect your response, click on the radio button or the response again. To change your response, click on a different radio button or a different response.

 **Play the CD to listen to the recording that goes with this item.**

4 Click on the "Next" button to go to the next item. The timer for the listening part will continue running.

The recordings for this item type run for approximately 20–70 seconds. Each recording will play only once. There are two to three *Select missing word* items in PTE Academic, depending on the combination of items in a given test. They are presented together in a single block.

6

Listening

Scoring

Your response is scored as either correct or incorrect. No credit is given for no response or an incorrect response. This item type affects the scoring of the following:

Overall score			✔
Communicative skills			
Listening	✔	Speaking	
Reading		Writing	
Enabling skills			
Grammar		Spelling	
Oral fluency		Vocabulary	
Pronunciation		Written discourse	

Listening skills

Select missing word tests your listening skills in an academic environment. Below are the key skills tested:

- identifying the topic, theme or main idea
- identifying words and phrases appropriate to the context
- understanding academic vocabulary
- inferring the meaning of unfamiliar words
- comprehending explicit and implicit information
- comprehending concrete and abstract information
- following an oral sequencing of information
- predicting how a speaker may continue
- forming a conclusion from what a speaker says
- comprehending variations in tone, speed, accent

Your speaking and writing skills are not tested by this item type, and your reading skills are only used to read the instructions and the response options.

Strategies

Before listening

- Read the instructions. The first sentence of the instructions describes the topic of the recording. Knowing the topic of the recording helps you prepare for it.

While listening

- Focus on the general content of the recording. You need to understand the main points as well as the details.

- Pay attention to the audio progress indicator. This helps you anticipate the end of the recording.

After listening

- Read the response options and select the correct one.
- Think about the option you have chosen. Does it have the right meaning to be the missing word? Is it the right part of speech to be the missing word?
- Attempt the item if you are not sure which is the correct response. It is better to attempt the item than to leave it unanswered.

Practice

Below is a *Select missing word* item for you to respond to.

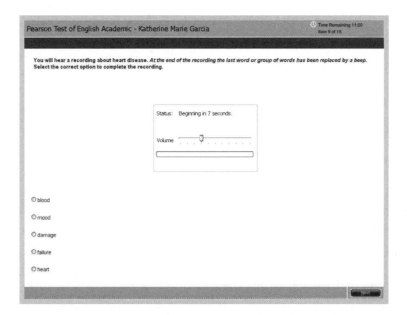

19 **Listen to the recording only once. Then select the correct response.**

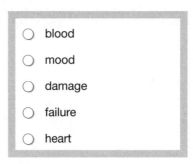

- ○ blood
- ○ mood
- ○ damage
- ○ failure
- ○ heart

Remember, during PTE Academic you will give your response by clicking on a response at a test delivery workstation.

6

Listening

Answer key p.191 **Now check the Answer key.**

Highlight incorrect words

Task

Highlight incorrect words is an item type that tests your ability to listen for and point out the differences between a recording and a transcription. It assesses both listening and reading skills. The image below shows the item type.

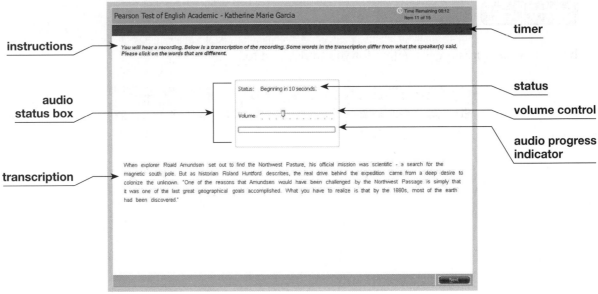

PTE Academic: Highlight incorrect words

Below are the features of *Highlight incorrect words*.

1 Instructions are presented at the top of the computer screen.

> *You will hear a recording. Below is a transcription of the recording. Some words in the transcription differ from what the speaker(s) said. Please click on the words that are different.*

2 In the audio status box, the status will count down from 10 seconds. Then a recording will play automatically.

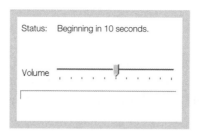

Status: Beginning in 10 seconds.

Volume

The audio progress indicator represents the entire duration of the recording. So if the recording is short, the bar moves faster. If the recording is long, the bar moves slower.

The status will change to "Playing." To adjust the volume of the recording, move the slider left to decrease and right to increase. You can adjust the volume at any time while the recording is playing. The audio progress indicator features a blue bar that will gradually move to the right as the recording continues. When the recording finishes, the status will change to "Completed."

3 A transcription of the recording with up to seven deliberate errors follows.

> When explorer Roald Amundsen set out to find the Northwest Pasture, his official mission was scientific—a search for the magnetic south pole. But as historian Roland Huntford describes, the real drive behind the expedition came from a deep desire to colonize the unknown. "One of the reasons that Amundsen would have been challenged by the Northwest Passage is simply that it was one of the last great geographical goals accomplished. What you have to realize is that by the 1880s, most of the earth had been discovered."

To respond, click on the words in the transcription that differ from what you hear on the recording. Each word you select will be highlighted in yellow. To deselect a word, click on the word again.

 Play the CD to listen to the recording that goes with this item.

4 Click on the "Next" button to go to the next item. The timer for the listening part will continue running.

The recordings for this item type run for approximately 15–50 seconds. Each recording will play only once. Any word in the transcription may differ from the recordings. There are two to three *Highlight incorrect words* items in PTE Academic, depending on the combination of items in a given test. They are presented together in a single block.

6

Listening

Scoring

Each selected word is scored as either correct or incorrect. If all the selected words are correct, you receive the maximum score points for this item type. If one or more selected words are incorrect, partial credit scoring applies. This is the third of three item types where you can lose points if you choose any incorrect options. For any wrong options chosen 1 point is deducted, whilst correct options are given 1 point. Make sure you are confident in your choices. This item type affects the scoring of the following:

Overall score			✔
Communicative skills			
Listening	✔	Speaking	
Reading	✔	Writing	
Enabling skills			
Grammar		Spelling	
Oral fluency		Vocabulary	
Pronunciation		Written discourse	

Listening and reading skills

Highlight incorrect words is an integrated skills item type that tests both your listening and reading skills in an academic environment. Below are the key skills tested:

Listening

- identifying errors in a transcription
- understanding academic vocabulary
- following an oral sequencing of information
- comprehending variations in tone, speed, accent

Reading

- understanding academic vocabulary
- following a logical or chronological sequence of events
- reading a text under timed conditions
- matching written text to speech

Your speaking and writing skills are not tested by this item type.

Strategies

Before listening

- Skim the transcription quickly. This will help you understand what you hear.
- Position the cursor at the beginning of the text so that you are prepared to click and select.
- Watch the status in the audio status box, and be prepared to follow the text with the cursor when the recording begins.

While listening

- Focus on identifying words in the transcription.
- Move the cursor along the text as you hear the words. Be prepared to click on any word which does not match what is said.
- Do not make guesses. Only click on a word in the text when you are sure it is different from the word in the recording.

Practice

Below is a *Highlight incorrect words* item for you to respond to.

Pearson Test of English Academic - Katherine Marie Garcia

Time Remaining 08:12
Item 11 of 15

You will hear a recording. Below is a transcription of the recording. Some words in the transcription differ from what the speaker(s) said. Please click on the words that are different.

Status: Beginning in 10 seconds.

Volume

So far in our discussion of chemical equations we have assumed that these reactions only go in one direction, the forward direction, from left to right as we read it in the equation. That's why our arrowhead points from left to right: reactants react together to make products. However, this is not exactly how things occur in reality. In fact, practically every chemical reaction is reversible, meaning the products can also react together to reform the reactants that they were made of. So instead of writing that single arrow facing from right to top, a more appropriate symbol would be a double arrow, one going from left to right and one going from right to left. Reactants are continually - continuously - reacting to form produce. But at the same time as those products are formed, they remake the reactants. They're both going simultaneously, forming each other. This is what we would call a state of equality.

Next

21 **Listen to the recording only once. As you listen, circle the words in the transcription that differ from what the speaker says.**

So far in our discussion of chemical equations we have assumed that these reactions only go in one direction, the forward direction, from left to right as we read it in the equation. That's why our arrowhead points from left to right: reactants react together to make products. However, this is not exactly how things occur in reality. In fact, practically every chemical reaction is reversible, meaning the products can also react together to reform the reactants that they were made of. So instead of writing that single arrow facing from right to top, a more appropriate symbol would be a double arrow, one going from left to right and one going from right to left. Reactants are continually, continuously reacting to form produce. But at the same time as those products are formed, they remake the reactants. They're both going simultaneously, forming each other. This is what we would call a state of equality.

Remember, during PTE Academic you will give your response by clicking on words at a test delivery workstation.

Answer key **p.192** **Now check the Answer key.**

Write from dictation

Task

Write from dictation is an item type that tests your ability to understand and remember a sentence you hear, and then write it exactly as you hear it using correct spelling. It assesses both listening and writing skills. The image below shows the item type.

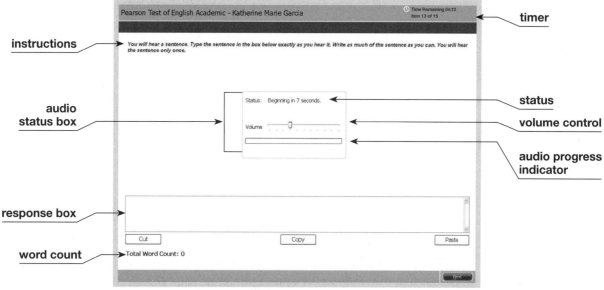

PTE Academic: Write from dictation

Below are the features of *Write from dictation*.

1 Instructions are presented at the top of the computer screen.

> *You will hear a sentence. Type the sentence in the box below exactly as you hear it. Write as much of the sentence as you can. You will hear the sentence only once.*

2 In the audio status box, the status will count down from seven seconds. Then a recording will play automatically.

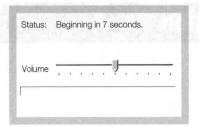

Status: Beginning in 7 seconds.

Volume

The audio progress indicator represents the entire duration of the recording. So if the recording is short, the bar moves faster. If the recording is long, the bar moves slower.

The status will change to "Playing." To adjust the volume of the recording, move the slider left to decrease and right to increase. You can adjust the volume at any time while the recording is playing. The audio progress indicator features a blue bar that will gradually move to the right as the recording continues. When the recording finishes, the status will change to "Completed."

3 A response box follows.

Cut   Copy   Paste
Total Word Count: 0

Use this space to type the sentence. You can select text within the response box with the mouse, and use the "Cut," "Copy" and "Paste" buttons to edit your response. The "Total Word Count" keeps track of the number of words written and updates as you type.

22   **Play the CD to listen to the recording that goes with this item.**

4 Click on the "Next" button to go to the next item. The timer for the listening part will continue running.

The recordings for this item type run for approximately three to five seconds. Each recording will play only once. There are three to four *Write from dictation* items in PTE Academic, depending on the combination of items in a given test. They are presented together in a single block.

Scoring

Your score on *Write from dictation* is based on the following factor:

➤ **Content:** Does your response include all the words in the sentence, and only these words?

Content is scored by counting the number of correct words in your response.

160

If all the words are right and spelled correctly, you receive the maximum score points for this item type. If one or more words are incorrect, partial credit scoring applies. This item type affects the scoring of the following:

Overall score			✔
Communicative skills			
Listening	✔	Speaking	
Reading		Writing	✔
Enabling skills			
Grammar		Spelling	
Oral fluency		Vocabulary	
Pronunciation		Written discourse	

Listening and writing skills

Write from dictation is an integrated skills item type that tests both your listening and writing skills in an academic environment. Below are the key skills tested:

Listening

- understanding academic vocabulary
- following an oral sequencing of information
- comprehending variations in tone, speed, accent

Writing

- writing from dictation
- using correct spelling

Your speaking skills are not tested by this item type, and your reading skills are only used to read the instructions.

Strategies

Before listening

- Place the cursor in the response box so that you are prepared to type.

While listening

- Focus on the meaning of the sentence. This will help you remember it.
- Write the sentence immediately.

    — If you can type fast, type the sentence directly into the response box.
    — If you can write fast, write the sentence, or take notes using the Erasable Noteboard Booklet and pen. Type the sentence into the response box after listening.

6

Listening

161

- Finish typing or writing the sentence before correcting any mistakes you make.

After listening

- Re-read the sentence and correct any grammar, spelling, punctuation or capitalization mistakes.

Practice

Below is a *Write from dictation* item for you to respond to.

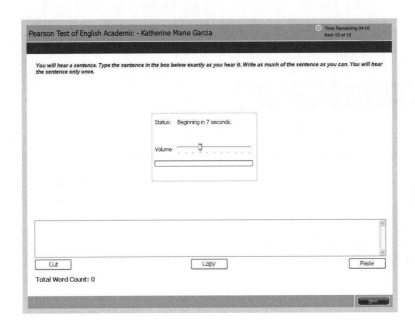

 23 **Listen to the recording only once. Then write the sentence exactly as you hear it in the space provided below.**

> Remember, during PTE Academic you will type in your response at a test delivery workstation.

....

....

....

Answer key **p.192** **Now check the Answer key.**

Improving general listening skills

Effective listening

Effective listening, in both everyday and test situations, requires attention to the four areas listed below. Although not all of these areas will be tested in PTE Academic, improving your skills in each area will help your general language proficiency and improve your overall performance in the test.

➤ **Context**
- Identify the context in which a speaking activity takes place by recognizing words, phrases or commonly used utterances, or exchanges in different contexts. For example, the expression "What's the special today?" might be heard in a restaurant. "We begin this evening with a discussion of Chapter 3" could be heard in a lecture hall.

➤ **Topic and gist**
- Understand the topic and logical development of a speaking activity.

  — Recognize the key words or phrases which provide clues to the topic, for example, "environmental problem" or "scientific solution."
  — Understand the key expressions which help structure a speech. For example, recognize signposting words and phrases such as "first," "finally," "Our last point is about …." Recognize cohesive devices such as "so that," "if … then …," "only if," "consequently."

➤ **Specific information**
- Identify the key words or phrases that refer to specific information. For example, understand references to day, time and place, key points in an argument, or facts in a presentation.
- Identify and ask for specific information, using clarification techniques. For example, "I'm sorry, could you remind me about where we're meeting?"

➤ **Speaker's point of view**
- Understand the speaker's point of view. For example, recognize words and phrases such as "I think," "In my opinion."
- Understand the speaker's feelings by recognizing stress, tone, intonation and body language that are used to convey emotion. For example, saying "told" with a higher tone in "I told you" may indicate impatience. Stressing "offer" in "The student did not even offer a reason for …" may indicate indignation and disapproval of the student's behavior.

6

Listening

163

Understanding your strengths and weaknesses

Improving your listening skills starts with an understanding of your own strengths and weaknesses. This will allow you to concentrate on areas which need to be improved in general, or specifically as preparation for taking PTE Academic. Use the checklist below to assess your current listening skills and to decide on priority areas for improvement.

Effective listening	My current proficiency level			Priority for improvement
	High	Medium	Low	
Context				
I can understand the context in which a speaking activity takes place.				
Topic and gist				
I can recognize the key words or phrases which provide clues to the topic or gist.				
I can understand the key expressions which help structure the speech.				
Specific information				
I can identify the key words or phrases about specific information.				
I can identify specific gaps in my listening comprehension, and ask questions appropriately to clarify what was said.				
Speaker's point of view				
I can understand the speaker's point of view and feelings by recognizing relevant words and phrases.				
I can understand the speaker's feelings by listening for stress, tone and intonation, and by noticing body language.				

Developing your listening skills

Follow the suggestions below to improve your general listening skills.

➤ **Listen more. Look for opportunities to hear English.**
- Join English-speaking groups to listen to English in a range of authentic settings.
  - Participants in these activities often come from different regions, so you have a chance to listen to different accents.
  - Note informal and idiomatic expressions that you hear.
- Attend face-to-face presentations, lectures and discussion sessions that are held in English. Some English language learning websites offer access to events that you can participate in online.

— Pay particular attention to the ways in which speakers organize their presentations, how they express their points of view and how they respond to questions.

— Listen closely to questions to check the structures that are used and the ways in which polite questions are formulated.

- Listen to news broadcasts. Aim to understand the topic of each news item without necessarily knowing the meaning of every word.
- Use free Internet listening resources and activities on educational websites for learners of English as a foreign or second language (EFL or ESL).
- Watch or listen to TV or Internet programs that you are interested in. Quiz programs, for example, provide useful practice in listening to questions and responses.
- Observe native English speakers and listen to the language used for different purposes in different contexts. Pay attention to their body language, gestures and informal expressions.

➤ Practice your listening skills.
- Use online listening comprehension courses or textbooks and CDs to practice regularly. Work through the questions and check your answers with the answer key. Listen again to check your understanding when necessary.
- Practice predicting what will come next when you are listening.

— Think about how you predict what you will hear when you are listening in your first language. Then try it out in English. Pause the audio recording in the middle of a sentence. Ask yourself what might come next. Then play the recording to check.

- Take an online or classroom-based listening course. This will allow you to get listening practice that is tailored to your proficiency level and needs.

Listening strategies

➤ Be prepared to make inferences.
- Infer the meanings of unfamiliar words using context clues. You can get a general idea of what is said without understanding everything you hear.

➤ Use clarification and confirmation techniques.
- Use clarification techniques to check for information. For example, "What time did you say?" or "Can you repeat the population figures?" Ask specifically for the information you need.
- Use confirmation techniques to ensure that you are getting the message correctly. For example, in making arrangements, you might say "Right, that's lunch at 12:30." This gives you and your conversation partner the chance to confirm that you have understood correctly.

Sources of listening material

- Online English courses or textbooks with accompanying CDs or DVDs provide samples of authentic or adapted listening materials. Choose materials which have written scripts and/or answers to questions, so that you can check your listening comprehension.

6

Listening

- English-speaking groups offer the opportunity to practice both listening and speaking skills. Search for global groups on the Internet and find out about local clubs in your area.
- The Internet offers the opportunity to listen to a wide range of genres including presentations, lectures, descriptions, stories, commentaries and more.
- Television programs offer a range of situations in which authentic and scripted language is used. Some programs are subtitled, which can be helpful for overall comprehension and for exposure to a wide range of topics and language.
- Radio broadcasts provide listening material on a range of topics. News broadcasts provide exposure to short, well-organized presentations on a number of topics. Stories or dramas provide practice in following the gist of description or dialogue, including recognition of how emotions are conveyed in speech.
- Face-to-face public lectures or short talks are usually well-structured and are sometimes accompanied by written outlines, which can be helpful for both listening and speaking practice.

Preparing for PTE Academic

To prepare for PTE Academic, you should practice the listening skills that you will be assessed on in the test.

- Read Chapter 6 of the *Official Guide* to obtain information on all aspects of the listening item types in the test and practice responding to the example items.
- Use the CD-ROM included with the *Official Guide* to gain further practice in responding to listening items.
- Use the PTE Academic Tutorial available at www.pearsonpte.com to learn how to respond to these items in the actual test.
- Take a practice test available at www.pearsonpte.com.

Refer to the section "Resources" in Chapter 2 of the *Official Guide* for further information.

Answer key and transcripts

Task items

Chapter 3

Speaking

p. 45 **Repeat sentence**

Transcript

It's a good idea to begin your dissertation with a review of the literature.

p. 55 **Re-tell lecture**

Transcript

It's now well established that real and active participation in development has many positives for women—and as a flow-on—for households, children and communities, and um even in the most remote communities there has at least been discussion of women's rights to participate, and women are having a voice. Let's not be naïve about this—there is still a long way to go!

Many of the women we have talked about today have become more financially independent, or at least less financially dependent, they have developed their skills, their economic potential, and their participation has provided opportunities for increased gender equity for—I can't read what I've ... here for improved resources and conditions and these have enabled girls to go to school, all of which will have a profound impact on future generations of women.

p. 61 **Answer short question**

newspaper, a newspaper, newspapers

Transcript

What type of periodical is published on a daily basis?

Chapter 5

Reading

p. 91 ## Multiple-choice, choose single answer

One present indicator of climate change in Australia is _____

- ○ environmental activists.
- ○ gas emissions.
- ○ carbon dioxide.
- ● drought.

p. 96 ## Multiple-choice, choose multiple answers

According to the text, which of the following statements can be concluded about primary classes in the Turks and Caicos Islands?

- ☑ Multigrade classes are mainly found in smaller schools.
- ☐ Most primary pupils are in multigrade classes.
- ☐ Parents can choose to send their child to a multigrade school.
- ☑ Most primary pupils are in mixed ability classes.
- ☐ Multigrade classes are for the youngest three grades.

p. 101 ## Re-order paragraphs

Doctor Byron has long held that there is a link between diet and acne.

He convinced Professor Fitzgerald of the University of Hull to set up a study into this matter.

Professor Fitzgerald and his team studied more than 47000 women.

The women were asked to fill in a questionnaire about their diet and about their suffering from acne.

No link was found between acne and traditionally suspect food such as chocolate and chips.

p. 106 Reading: Fill in the blanks

Master of Science in Information Technology (MSc in IT). Our programme will develop your

| theoretical | knowledge of Computer Science and your problem-solving and

| analytical | skills, while enabling you to achieve the | ultimate |

qualification for the IT professional. The programme structure is extremely

| flexible |, enabling you to personalise your MSc through a wide range of

electives.

p. 110 Reading & writing: Fill in the blanks

The impact of a product recall can be wide-reaching, and will almost certainly extend beyond

the purely financial | considerations ▼ | of taking products off shelves. David Palmer,

director of product risk management for Aon Limited, points out, "It takes companies many

years to establish a strong brand name and | reputation ▼ | and it only takes one

product recall to bring it crashing down." Despite heightened awareness around product

recalls, and significant investment in product control, some businesses are still falling

| short ▼ | when it comes to implementing strategies to deal with a crisis.

Chapter 6 Listening

p. 124 Summarize spoken text

Transcript

I have chosen *The Search for Stability* as the title of my lectures, because I want to deal specifically with macroeconomics, the question of how we can keep the economy on a reasonably stable growth path. While there are disagreements about many aspects of economics, such as those dealing with efficiency, income distribution, or the role of the market versus the role of the state, I think there is widespread agreement across the political spectrum that stability is a good thing.

Economically, the first half of the 20th century was disfigured by the Great Depression of the 1930s, and the second half by the high inflation of the 1970s. No one wants a repeat of these episodes, nor of some of the other disruptions that have marked the past 60 years. To some, the word "stability" sounds unexciting, and probably more so if I use the term "economic stability." But stability is not just an economic concept; it has a profound impact on the lives of people. Instability can create havoc, damage institutions, and leave a legacy from which some families and nations will take many years to recover. For example, the rise of Nazism in Germany was helped by the preceding Weimar hyper-inflation. Fortunately, in Australia, we've had nothing like that, but the effects of the Depression left scars that lasted for lifetimes. Likewise, the effects of the big rise in unemployment and inflation in the 1970s have not fully passed out of our economy.

p. 130

Multiple-choice, choose multiple answers

According to the speaker, how are online news sources making the news industry more competitive?

- ■ There are more media options to choose from.
- ☐ More advertising revenue comes from online news articles.
- ☐ People care less about the national news.
- ☐ The national stations have taken over the online media market.
- ■ It is easier to get the news from outside sources.

Transcript

I hate to say it, but probably the best thing that could happen right now is a little consolidation, because one of the reasons that we have so many news sources out there is because up until recently, the local newspaper in everybody's town was the only newspaper they got, pretty much. Well, now, if you're consuming news online, then what's the difference between the local newspaper that I read in Kentucky versus the one that the guy reads in Dallas, or the one that somebody reads out in North Dakota? And it turns out that if you did a comparison, I'm just making this figure up, but I'm going to guess that it's about 90% similar stuff. I mean, when you take out High School football scores, restaurant reviews, and local social gatherings, and you just have, like, you know, regional and national stuff in there, you really can get that stuff from anywhere. And so, I think what's happened is that a lot of these newspapers and local TV stations don't realize that now they're all in direct competition with not only each other but the nationals as well.

170

p. 135

Fill in the blanks

Well, sometimes, representatives of a company make misstatements. They get

something wrong regarding | corporate | policy. And there, sometimes

the problem is just letting people upfront know that sometimes this happens, and

| apologize / apologise | quickly when it does. What some companies do as an alternative

is have ... | hobbyists | , aficionados run the discussion boards and then

representatives participate in that, but then they have much less | liability |

as far as I can tell.

Transcript

Well, sometimes, representatives of a company make misstatements. They get something wrong regarding corporate policy. And there, sometimes the problem is just letting people upfront know that sometimes this happens, and apologize quickly when it does. What some companies do as an alternative is have ... hobbyists, aficionados run the discussion boards and then representatives participate in that, but then they have much less liability as far as I can tell.

p. 140

Highlight correct summary

○ Recent research shows that when customers are dissatisfied with service or products, they usually inform the company of their complaint. They tend to talk about their negative experience with others if the company doesn't respond to their initial complaint.

◉ Recent research shows that nearly one third of dissatisfied customers will share a negative retail experience with someone else. Nearly half of the people surveyed said that they had avoided a store due to another individual's negative experience.

○ Recent research shows that nearly 80% of customers who had a bad experience with a company will share that experience with people they know. Furthermore, 70% of people who hear about another individual's negative experience will avoid a store based on what they've heard.

○ Recent research shows that most customers have had a negative experience with a company at some time. When this happens, the majority tend to avoid the store in future. More seriously for the companies, however, between 32 and 36 out of every hundred customers will tell others about that experience, and exaggerate the story.

Wharton Marketing Professor Stephen Hoch, who suffered through this scenario first-hand during a recent shopping trip, says customers are bound to talk about these kinds of experiences. And, according to new Wharton research, such word-of-mouth communication should be a big cause of concern to retailers. Results of The Retail Customer Dissatisfaction Study 2006—conducted by The Jay H. Baker Retailing Initiative at Wharton and The Verde Group, a Toronto consulting firm, in the weeks before and after Christmas 2005—show that only 6% of shoppers who experienced a problem with a retailer contacted the company, but 31% went on to tell friends, family or colleagues what happened. Of those, 8% told one person, another 8% told two people, but 6% told six or more people. "Even though these shoppers don't share their pain with the store, they do share their pain with other people. Apparently, quite a few other people," says Hoch. Overall, if 100 people have a bad experience, a retailer stands to lose between 32 and 36 current or potential customers, according to the study. The complaints have an even greater impact on shoppers who were not directly involved as the story spreads and is embellished, researchers found. Almost half of those surveyed, 48%, reported they have avoided a store in the past because of someone else's negative experience.

p. 145

Multiple-choice, choose single answer

What does the speaker believe is likely to happen in the future?

⦿ The media will be owned by a small number of corporations.

◯ The public will eventually pay for the funding of the media.

◯ The media will be run primarily for the purpose of making profit.

◯ Most media analysts will continue to report what they see.

Transcript

It's, it's particularly harmful to democracy when media systems are in the hands of private tyrannies. I mean it's bad enough if the guys who you know, making shoes or cars, that's bad enough, but when it's control over the doctrinal system and information, that's much worse. That's why I think the stuff that's going on in telecommunications now is so, should really have a lot more attention than it does. I mean here's this huge system, you know, built at public expense, I mean you guys paid for it, you know, and as usual being handed over to private power now that it's profitable, and it's very likely I think most media analysts with their heads screwed on see and indeed even report that it's going to end up in the hands of the half a dozen mega corporations internationally.

p. 150

Select missing word

◯ they become dedicated

◯ they get exhausted

172

○ they're rather improved

◉ they're quite competent

○ they're quite indifferent

Transcript

The Surgical Simulation Project is designed to provide an environment where people can practice doing surgery where the surgeon can see and feel a scenario that they would be seeing and interacting with in the actual surgery. It's sort of like flight simulation in that if your pilot is flying a 747, you would like to have had that pilot fly a simulator until they're quite competent.

p. 154

Highlight incorrect words

When explorer Roald Amundsen set out to find the Northwest Pasture, his official mission was scientific—a search for the magnetic south pole. But as historian Roland Huntford describes, the real drive behind the expedition came from a deep desire to colonize the unknown. "One of the reasons that Amundsen would have been challenged by the Northwest Passage is simply that it was one of the last great geographical goals accomplished. What you have to realize is that by the 1880s, most of the earth had been discovered."

Transcript

When explorer Roald Amundsen set out to find the Northwest Passage, his official mission was scientific—a search for the magnetic north pole. But as historian Roland Huntford describes, the real drive behind the expedition came from a deep desire to conquer the unknown. "One of the reasons that Amundsen would have been inspired by the Northwest Passage is simply that it was one of the last great geographical goals unaccomplished. What you have to realize is that by the 1870s, most of the earth had been discovered."

p. 159

Write from dictation

The cart carries a single object.

Transcript

The cart carries a single object.

Practice items

Chapter 3

Speaking

p. 44 Read aloud

Compare your response with the three sample responses on the Audio CD. Each one was given by a PTE Academic test taker. They illustrate the CEF levels of competence C1, B2 and B1. See the Appendix for information on the CEF language descriptors.

C1 The content of this response is excellent. This response is spoken at a conversational rate of speech and demonstrates good phrasing and smooth word emphasis. Additionally, there are no hesitations, repetitions or false starts. The pronunciation of most vowels and consonants is standard. Word and phrase stress is also appropriate.

B2 The content of this response is excellent. Disconnected phrasing and uneven rate of speech prevents the response from receiving full credit for fluency. There are no hesitations, repetitions or false starts. The pronunciation of several vowels and consonants is not standard and there are also several word and phrase stress errors.

B1 The content of this response is weak. Some words in the text are omitted, and some words that are not in the text are added. Disconnected phrasing and uneven rate of speech prevents the response from receiving full credit for fluency. There is also a hesitation and false start. Additionally, missing or incorrect pronunciation of vowels and consonants makes several words and phrases incomprehensible to most regular speakers of English.

Transcript

Photography's gaze widened during the early years of the twentieth century and, as the snapshot camera became increasingly popular, the making of photographs became increasingly available to a wide cross-section of the public. The British people grew accustomed to, and were hungry for, the photographic image.

Repeat sentence

p. 49

Compare your response with the three sample responses on the Audio CD. Each one was given by a PTE Academic test taker. They illustrate the CEF levels of competence C1, B2 and B1. See the Appendix for information on the CEF language descriptors.

C1 The content of this response is excellent. The response is spoken at a conversational rate of speech and the phrasing is appropriate. There are no repetitions, hesitations or false starts. Additionally, vowels and consonants are pronounced correctly.

B2 The content of this response is excellent. Uneven phrasing prevents the response from receiving full credit for fluency. There are no hesitations, repetitions or false starts. Minor pronunciation and stress errors do not affect intelligibility.

B1 The content of this response is weak. Some words in the sentence are omitted, and some words that are not in the sentence are added. The rate of speech is uneven and there is one hesitation. However, most words are spoken in continuous phrases. Some consonants are not pronounced and other consonants and vowels are mispronounced. Stress is placed incorrectly on some words.

Transcript ··

Please submit your work electronically, if you can.

---

p. 54 # Describe image

Compare your response with the three sample responses on the Audio CD. Each one was given by a PTE Academic test taker. They illustrate the CEF levels of competence C1, B2 and B1. See the Appendix for information on the CEF language descriptors.

C1

> The graph shows the development in comparing more or less developed countries, which, um, it compares to date against the amount by which it develops. And it shows that the less developed regions by year from 1950 to 2050 will have a significant or wider development compared to more developed regions.

The content of this response is fairly good. The major aspects of the graph and relationships between elements are accurately discussed. However, the test taker does not mention population growth, rather the test taker says the graph is showing the amount of development in developing and developed countries. The response is spoken at a conversational rate of speech and the phrasing is appropriate. This response demonstrates good control of grammar with very few errors. The vocabulary used is precise and appropriate for the context. The pronunciation is standard and all words are easily understandable. Stress is placed correctly on common words. This response is 22 seconds long.

B2

> This graph shows that in less developed regions, the population has grown in the last years. Meanwhile the developed regions has maintained their growth even in the last. The projections show that the the more developed regions will will continue being stable. Meanwhile the less developed regions will continue their grow to almost nine bil—

The content of this response is just adequate. While the response describes major aspects of the graph, the content is repetitive and several key details are not included. The response is spoken at an acceptable rate and in continuous phrases. There are several hesitations, false starts and repetitions which prevent the response from receiving full credit for fluency.

Sentence structure is basic and there are obvious grammar and vocabulary errors. The pronunciation of several vowels and consonants is not standard and there are also several word and phrase stress errors. This response is 40 seconds long.

B1

> The grap shows the grow in more and less to (unintelligible) countries from 1950 to 2050.

The content of this response is weak. There is no discussion of the relationships between elements of the graph, and only major aspects are described. Fluency is negatively affected by uneven rhythm, poor phrasing and multiple hesitations. The vocabulary is basic and limited to words that appear on the graph. This response demonstrates limited control over simple grammatical structures. Certain consonants are consistently pronounced in a non-native manner, which requires the listener to adjust to the accent. Stress placement on common words is not standard. This response is 13 seconds long.

p. 60

Re-tell lecture

Compare your response with the three sample responses on the Audio CD. Each one was given by a PTE Academic test taker. They illustrate the CEF levels of competence C1, B2 and B1. See the Appendix for information on the CEF language descriptors.

C1

> The lecturer was just talking about a rocket that was, um, that is launched by the Russians. Um yep. In the lecture he was just mentioning that this rocket was going to be launched to the International Space Station. And, um, what was interesting about this was not the rocket itself but that, um, the Russians actually developed the rocket ages ago and they are still using the same rocket, um, nowadays.

The content of this response is excellent. The topic has been accurately discussed and the supporting points are included. The response is spoken at a conversational rate of speech and the phrasing is appropriate. Word emphasis is smooth. This response demonstrates good control of grammar. The vocabulary used is appropriate for the context and varied. Also, simple connectors and cohesive devices are used. The pronunciation of most vowels and consonants is standard. Word and phrase stress is also appropriate. This response is 35 seconds long.

B2

> Uh. In this picture it is a rocket. Uh. And it is, um, it is a rocket which can have for space station which is built by Russian 30 years ago. And what is, uh, what is drawing our attention is the back field. Uh, half ago, uh, half a century ago, the Russian has have the, uh, technology to, uh, support a rocket.

The content of this response is good. While the response includes some main points, other key information from the lecture is omitted. Uneven phrasing, several hesitations, repetitions and false starts prevent this response from receiving full credit for fluency. Language use is weak. Basic grammar and vocabulary errors are present. The pronunciation of several vowels and consonants is not standard. Several word and phrase stress errors require the listener to adjust to the accent. This response is 35 seconds long.

35

B1

> Um. Very old type of locket type like a screw, a screw (unintelligible). That rocket is made in (unintelligible). It is a very old type of locket. Um. There are characteristic of the back part of the locket is are a kind of very old fashion. And, uh, but it is still used in, uh, used now.

The content of this response is weak. While the response includes some main points, other key information from the lecture is misrepresented. Fluency is affected by uneven rhythm, poor phrasing, multiple hesitations, false starts and repetitions. This response demonstrates limited control over simple grammatical structures. The vocabulary is basic and the word choice is repetitive. Certain vowels and consonants are consistently mispronounced. Stress placement on common words is not standard. This response is 34 seconds long.

Transcript

Now you can't have escaped hearing about Sputnik over the last few days—the newspapers have mentioned it. There was a symbol on Google—I don't know how many of you used Google on Thursday but there was a little symbol for Sputnik there. What we're looking at is the machine that launched Sputnik. Well, not quite: this is called a Soyuz rocket, and it's what takes the crews up to the International Space Station. It's the rocket that the Russians still use today. It's not that view that I'm interested in, it's the back view of the rocket. And the back view of this rocket is indistinguishable in almost every regard from the rocket that began the space age half a century ago. Because what the Russians have done is, they found a rocket that worked half a century ago, and they've stuck with it.

p. 64

Answer short question

> (the) equator or (the) equatorial line

Transcript

What is the demarcation point that divides the Earth into a Northern Hemisphere and a Southern Hemisphere?

Chapter 4

Writing

p. 77

Summarize written text

Compare your response with the three sample responses below. Each one was given by a PTE Academic test taker. They illustrate the CEF levels of competence C1, B2 and B1. See the Appendix for information on the CEF language descriptors.

C1

> Legal rights and safeguards lead to long-lived investments by individuals, which has a far higher impact on raising living standards of countries than these countries' natural resources.

The content of this response is excellent. The topic has been accurately discussed and the supporting points are included. The grammar follows standard conventions. All words are spelled correctly. The vocabulary used is appropriate for the context. The response is one complete sentence.

B2

> Natural resources such as proper lands to be cultivated and ample energy help a country becoming rich, but laws and stable political situations are more important in developing a nation.

The content of this response is adequate, although the summary does not demonstrate a complete understanding of the main point of the passage. Rather, the response summarizes a supporting point. The vocabulary used is appropriate for the context and contains one spelling mistake. The response is one complete sentence.

B1

> Variaty reason affect our wealth may involved political and legislation requirment on short-term and long-term investment.

The content of this response is weak. While the information provided in the response is relevant, the response is not an accurate summary of the passage. Missing or incorrect use of prepositions and verbs compromises understanding and prevents the response from receiving full credit for grammar. The vocabulary used is appropriate for the context. There are two spelling errors. Although weakly constructed, the response is one complete sentence.

p. 82

Write essay

Compare your response with the three sample responses below. Each one was given by a PTE Academic test taker. They illustrate the CEF levels of competence C1, B2 and B1. See the Appendix for information on the CEF language descriptors.

C1

Tobacco is one of the most widely-used drugs of the world. Over a billion adults legally smoke tobacco every day. Tobacco is slowing taking a billion people in the world towards doom. The long term health costs are high for smokers, who suffer from various heart and lung diseases, reduced concentration and continually diminishing immunity.

Non-smokers, accompanying smokers or those who are in their close vicinity, also become "Passive" smokers and bear the toll of various inevitable diseases as they inhale the smoke which has an ill-effect on their respiratory systems. Thus, the health costs are high—for smokers themselves, and for wider community in terms of health care costs and lost productivity.

There has been awareness among people from many years, about the ill-effects of smoking and various campaigns run by the government, NGOs and local bodies to encourage people to quit smoking but the result have not been impressive. The solution is to nip the problem in the bud. School authorities and parents should keep a close eye so that children dont start to smoke because they think it is "cool". They should be made aware about the harmful effects of smoking.

Government could play a vital role too. Smoking should not be high-hand in advertisements and movie commercials which have a huge impact on people. It could levy high taxes on tobacco products to keep people away from its reach. Rules for checking children buying such products should be made stringent.

The onus to protect from such products also lie on individuals as will-power always does the trick. The knowledge of importance of being healthy has to be realized from within. It goes a long way to check the problem. Thus, the solution requires both legitimate action of Government and strong individual decisions to eliminate the problem.

This essay answers the question on topic. The roles of the government and the individual are well explained and supporting details are provided. There is good development of ideas and a logical structure. The main ideas are introduced in the first paragraph and the test taker's answer to the question is restated in the conclusion. General linguistic and vocabulary ranges are excellent. The vocabulary is precise and expresses subtleties and nuances. Idioms are also used appropriately. Minor grammatical errors prevent this response from receiving full credit for grammar usage and mechanics, although the intended meaning of the sentences is clear. Spelling is excellent. This essay is 300 words long.

B2

These days, statistics have shown that all around the world, over a billion adults legally smoke tobacco every day. Also, these numbers are expected to increase if nothing is done. It takes two to stop the numbers arising and therefore, the government and the smokers have to cooperate to make the country smoke-free.

The government should control the amount of smokers as the rising numbers could cause lost productivity and an increase in the crime rate. Campaigns should be created and advertisements using the mass media can actually help the smokers realize the disadvantages of smoking.

Besides that, smokers should also learn the gruesome facts on smoking. They should also realize that there's more to life than just smoking and that people near and dear to them could be affected from their habit. Studies have shown that people who have family members who are smokers can actually contract diseases such as cancer and other lung diseases.

Moreover, the increase in the number of smokers can actually mean that there would probably be an increase in crime rates as well. Smoking would then lead to other dangerous issues like drugs, prostitution, theft and even murder. Therefore, the government should act immediately to avoid further damage to society.

Certain smokers who want to quit can find it hard to do so and this is when the government's help can come in handy. That is by increasing the age limit for adolescents to smoke, increasing tax on tobacco products to make it a lot more expensive and also to provide support gropus for smokers who wish to quit.

In a nutshell, smoking is indeed a problem to the nation and it takes two to work it out. The government and the smokers themselves should work side by side to solve this issue.

This essay answers the question on topic and is well organized. There is a clear introduction, body and conclusion. In the body, the main ideas and details relate to the main point of the essay. However, some main ideas are not well supported with details, examples or explanations. There are obvious grammatical errors in sentences with complex structures. However, most grammatical errors do not hinder communication. Imprecise vocabulary prevents the response from receiving full credit for general linguistic range. The vocabulary range is good and clichés are used sparingly. There are no significant spelling errors. This essay is 300 words long.

B1

Cigarettes is one kind of tobacco which actually is one of the most widely-used drugs in the world. It is common in our everyday lives for that there are so many people smoking. However, nowadays more and more people pay much attention to their healthes, so the concept of "Smoking is unhealthy" is accepted by most people who reject in smoking. But there are still over a billion adults legally smoke tobacco every day that will costs a lot both for smokers themselves and for the wider community in terms of health care costs and lost productivity. Do governments have a legitimate role to legislate to protect citizens from the harmful effects of smoking? The answer will be yes for most of people. The first, smoking will do harm for smokers' health. The second, somking will do harm for people who are arround smokers such as families. And smoking is always a lead of a fire desaster. There are many reasons to restrict smoking. The point is how to do this. We know that every policy will make a consequence. If government shut down the tobacco facotories, it will definitely increase the price of cigarettes which will affect smokers—over a billion people—heavily because they won't change their habit just because there are fewer cigarettes. So I think the government should guide these people not t

This essay minimally answers the question on topic. The details and examples do not follow a well-developed logic that supports the test taker's position on the topic. The essay does not have a good organizational pattern. The introduction rephrases the topic, the body contains minimal supporting points and the conclusion is unfinished. Missing or incorrect use of verbs and nouns prevents this essay from receiving full credit for grammar usage and spelling. The vocabulary is limited and imprecise. Some words are not appropriate for the context. Spelling errors are numerous. This response is 227 words long.

Reading

p. 95

Multiple-choice, choose single answer

Which of the following can be inferred from the text?

○ Photography eventually made scientific expeditions more productive.

◉ Artists performed a variety of tasks in early scientific explorations.

○ Naturalists themselves were often talented artists.

○ Dissecting specimens was not as useful as taking them to England.

X ○ Photography eventually made scientific expeditions more productive.

This response is incorrect. Although the text implies that photography became a part of scientific expeditions, the text does not imply that photography made scientific expeditions more productive.

✓ ◉ Artists performed a variety of tasks in early scientific explorations.

This response is correct because the writer states that artists drew specimens, recorded dissections and sketched the people and places visited during early scientific explorations.

X ○ Naturalists themselves were often talented artists.

This response is incorrect because this point is not addressed in the text. The writer does not state whether naturalists were or were not talented artists.

X ○ Dissecting specimens was not as useful as taking them to England.

This response is incorrect because the writer states that naturalists preserved or dissected some of the specimens they found. The writer neither implies nor states whether preservation was more useful than dissection.

p. 100

Multiple-choice, choose multiple answers

Which of the following words have the same meaning in the passage as "residences"?

- ■ abodes
- ☐ amenities
- ☐ connections
- ■ dwellings
- ■ habitations
- ☐ hillsides
- ☐ terrain

✓ ■ abodes

This response is correct because "abodes" is a synonym for "residences." "Abodes" is described as "ancient," and since the residences were previously described as "ancient Bronze Age dwellings," it can be inferred that they are the same thing.

✗ ☐ amenities

This response is incorrect because "amenities" are things that the residences are "equipped out with" but not equivalent to.

✗ ☐ connections

This response is incorrect because "connections" is listed as one of the amenities provided by the residences.

✓ ■ dwellings

This response is correct because "dwellings" is a synonym for "residences." In the text, "dwellings" is used to further explain "residences."

✓ ■ habitations

This response is correct because "habitations" is a synonym for "residences." Also, the word "such" modifies "habitations," and links it to the "residences" mentioned in the previous sentence.

☐ hillsides

This response is incorrect because "hillsides" refers to the location of the residences, not the residences themselves.

 ☐ terrain

This response is incorrect because "terrain" is a type of landscape. Also, Spain's "unspoiled terrain" is contrasted in the passage with the "caves" that are used as residences.

p. 101 Re-order paragraphs

> Rogers felt that psychologists had the most important job in the world, because ultimately, it was not the physical sciences that would save us, but better interactions between human beings.
>
> The climate of openness and transparency he created in his sessions, if replicated within the family, the corporation, or in politics, would result in less angst and more constructive outcomes.
>
> But the key was a desire to really feel what the other person or party wanted and felt.
>
> Such a willingness, though not easy, could transform those involved.

> Rogers felt that psychologists had the most important job in the world, because ultimately, it was not the physical sciences that would save us, but better interactions between human beings.

This is the first text box because it introduces the topic and contains the main idea of the text. In addition, it attributes ideas to "Rogers," the only individual named in this text.

> The climate of openness and transparency he created in his sessions, if replicated within the family, the corporation, or in politics, would result in less angst and more constructive outcomes.

This is the second text box because it expands the main idea by describing the results of better interactions. Additionally, the pronouns "he" and "his" indicate that this person was named in a preceding text box.

> But the key was a desire to really feel what the other person or party wanted and felt.

This is the third text box because it describes how to obtain the described results. The coordinating conjunction "but," at the beginning of the text box, also indicates that information preceded this text box.

Such a willingness, though not easy, could transform those involved.

This is the fourth and last text box because it concludes the paragraph by suggesting overall results or consequences. In addition, "such a willingness" refers to the phrase, "a desire to really feel what the other person or party wanted and felt," indicating that this text box comes after the third text box.

p. 109 ## Reading: Fill in the blanks

Science blogs serve a dual purpose. First, they connect scientists to each other, **serving** as modern day intellectual salons. Even **formal** scientific papers are now beginning to **cite** blogs as references. Second, they connect scientists to the general **public**, offering a behind-the-scenes **look** at how science progresses.

p. 113 ## Reading & writing: Fill in the blanks

A Civil War reenactment is in part a memorial service. It is partly, too, a leisure activity. Furthermore most reenactors assert an educational import to the performance, and to develop their roles many pursue archival (1) **research** with a rare dedication. On the other hand Civil War reenactments are increasingly commercial (2) **spectacles**, with as many as fifty thousand Americans routinely gathering at (or near) historical Civil War battlefields to stage performances that purport to recreate the conflict, while hundreds of thousands more spectate.

I will show how theoretical issues of (3) **authenticity** arise as practical problems in the Civil War reenactment community by presenting my own observations from the 2006 Gettysburg reenactment and by (4) **relying** on a number of texts produced by participant-observers. In particular I will refer to Robert Lee Hodge, who was made famous by Tony Horwitz's 1996 book, Confederates in the Attic, and who served as a kind of Virgil to the author on his journey through a Confederate Valhalla. From these sources I will

> (5)   argue   ▼   that 'Living History' performances require an interpretive apparatus that takes genuine history as its authority, while remaining external to both participants and tourists, who may well be unaware of how closely their own involvement approximates genuine historical events.

Chapter 6   Listening

p. 128

Summarize spoken text

Compare your response with the three sample responses below. Each one was given by a PTE Academic test taker. They illustrate the CEF levels of competence C1, B2 and B1. See the Appendix for information on the CEF language descriptors.

C1

> In an interview with the CEO of Disney, the importance of locally produced content was raised: there is a global growth imperative, even with companies as well-established as Disney, not only to sell products in the language of a particular region, but also to make products locally relevant. Operating locally, companies can use local creativity and interests to enhance the relevancy of their products to their customers in that location.

The content of this response is excellent. The response is an accurate and detailed summary of the main point and several supporting points discussed in the lecture. The grammar follows standard conventions. The vocabulary used is appropriate for the context. All words are spelled correctly. This response is 70 words long.

B2

> As doing business in globalized world, Disney is trying to extend markets by targetting global grosses. This includes applying brand and non brand products. It is not just that strategy, the more important thing is by being locally relevant, moving people to market. By doing this, Disney is able to being creative locally. This means that Disney can pull them to its market by using their culture to attract them.

The content of this response is good. The main point has been discussed and supporting points are included. This response demonstrates limited grammatical control. Several errors on choice of word hinder understanding. There are two spelling errors. This response is 70 words long.

B1

> With the global ecnomic increasing sharply, we have to strong ourselves. I think we have ability to enter the global world and we will have a position. I believe the most important thing for us is how to send our production, our culture ana the belief to the global market , and how should we do to make these things accepted by the world and people lived in other contries. I have the strong belief that we will win.

The content of this response is weak. While the response contains information related to the lecture, the test taker misrepresents the main point. This response demonstrates weak grammatical control, which hinders understanding. The vocabulary is basic and imprecise. There are several spelling errors. This response is 79 words long, which is over the maximum length of 70 words.

Transcript

Interviewer: International expansion is also something that you've emphasised as CEO, and one interesting aspect of that has been a focus on locally-produced content. I wonder if you could talk about the ways in which, in a globalised world, in a global economy, locally-produced content is important for an iconic company like Disney.

Iger: Well, first of all, global growth is imperative for us. We are not only a very durable brand worldwide, but we are a very well-known brand, so I think we have the ability to not just succeed, but to grow and to thrive in many markets around the country for years to come. But in order to do so, it's not just about putting our product there, meaning taking something that's been made for another market, putting a local language track on it, and distributing it locally. It's about being locally relevant, and that means operating locally, meaning moving our people to markets so that they understand the markets, the culture, the interests. It's also about being creative locally: there's a lot of talent and a lot of creativity in many, many places around the world, and we have to tap into that content.

p. 133

Multiple-choice, choose multiple answers

Which of these countries use electronic voting machines?

☐   South Africa

■   India

☐   Indonesia

■   Holland

☐   United Kingdom

186

✗ ☐ South Africa

This response is incorrect because South Africa is not mentioned as having voting technology. It can be inferred from the speaker's statement, "everyone votes on good old paper ballots" that "everyone" refers to any nation not mentioned.

✓ ■ India

This response is correct because the speaker states that "the whole country of… India uses electronic voting machines."

✗ ☐ Indonesia

This response is incorrect because Indonesia is not mentioned as having voting technology. It can be inferred from the speaker's statement, "everyone votes on good old paper ballots" that "everyone" refers to any nation not mentioned.

✓ ■ Holland

This response is correct because the speaker states that Holland has voting machines.

✗ ☐ United Kingdom

This response is incorrect because the United Kingdom is not mentioned. It can be inferred from the speaker's statement, "everyone votes on good old paper ballots" that "everyone" refers to any nation not mentioned. Furthermore, the speaker says, "voting machines don't exist in most of the rest of the world, including Western Europe."

Transcript

Alright, a little bit of history. Well, the current debate we are having is a uniquely American phenomenon, uniquely American because voting machines don't exist in most of the rest of the world, including erm, western Europe, where one might think we'd find them. We really only have voting machines, I think about a third or a half of South America uses voting technology, uh, Holland does because there's a machine manufacturer there and the whole country of indria, India uses electronic voting machines, which is quite interesting. Those machines are made by the Indian government. But other than that, everyone votes on good old paper ballots.

p. 138   Fill in the blanks

OK, we're going to begin our lectures today on the [biological] basis of

mental life. Psychology was defined at the very beginning of the [existence]

of the science by William James as the science of mental life. As I [described]

last time, James argued that the whole purpose of psychology is to try to understand the

[cognitive] , emotional and motivational processes that [underlie]

human experience, thought and action. But because the brain is the [physical]

basis of the mind, the mind is what the brain does, James began his famous

[treatise] on psychology with a discussion of brain function.

Transcript

OK, we're going to begin our lectures today on the biological basis of mental life. Psychology was defined at the very beginning of the existence of the science by William James as the science of mental life. As I described last time, James argued that the whole purpose of psychology is to try to understand the cognitive, emotional and motivational processes that underlie human experience, thought and action. But because the brain is the physical basis of the mind, the mind is what the brain does, James began his famous treatise on psychology with a discussion of brain function.

p. 143   Highlight correct summary

○ The speaker explains the difference between electrochemistry and chemical metallurgy. The similarities and differences between the two are discussed, as well as factors that determine the differences.

○ The speaker explains the class objective and procedures to students. He also tells the class his background information and that they have the choice of attending a class either at 8 AM or 9 AM.

● The speaker gives his personal background related to the subject matter of the course. He discusses his background in education as well as research, and his experience teaching at this university.

○ The speaker tells about his experience at the University of Toronto and his PhD studies in electrochemistry there. He explains why he stayed in Canada for a longer period of time than the two years that he had planned.

○ The speaker explains the difference between electrochemistry and chemical metallurgy. The similarities and differences between the two are discussed, as well as factors that determine the differences.

This response is incorrect because the speaker does not explain the difference between electrochemistry and chemical metallurgy.

 ○ The speaker explains the class objective and procedures to students. He also tells the class his background information and that they have the choice of attending a class either at 8 AM or 9 AM.

This response is incorrect because the speaker does not explain the class objective and procedures. Although two class sections are mentioned, the reference is to the speaker's first teaching assignment instead of the current one.

 ● The speaker gives his personal background related to the subject matter of the course. He discusses his background in education as well as research, and his experience teaching at this university.

This response is correct because it accurately covers the key points made by the speaker.

 ○ The speaker tells about his experience at the University of Toronto and his PhD studies in electrochemistry there. He explains why he stayed in Canada for a longer period of time than the two years that he had planned.

This response is incorrect because the speaker says that he studied chemical metallurgy at the University of Toronto, not electrochemistry, and that he had planned to go back to Canada after one or two years.

Transcript

So let me begin by doing a little bit of background so that you know what's going on here. Uh, I was born in Canada. I went to the University of Toronto, and I studied chemical metallurgy. Chemical metallurgy, well you might say, "What's a person who studied chemical metallurgy doing teaching chemistry here?" Well, after my PhD I came here as a postdoctoral fellow in 1977. The plan was to stay for a year or two and go back to Canada. And I lost track of time. So I joined the faculty in 1978 and my first teaching assignment was 309-1 recitation. I had two sections: one met at 8 AM and one met at 9 AM. We don't have 8 AM sections; at least we haven't in recent years. Maybe it's time to revisit that. So my research is electrochemistry, that's why I'm teaching chemistry. Electrochemistry is the most important branch of chemistry. Why not? Find your passion and pursue it. So I'm interested in non-aqueous electrochemistry. I don't care about water. I'm interested in non-aqueous electrochemistry.

p. 149

Multiple-choice, choose single answer

According to the speaker, how did the Seven Years' War contribute to the start of the American Revolution?

- ○ The British Parliament refused consent for higher taxes.
- ◉ It led Britain to monitor more closely its colonial interests.
- ○ It caused the colonies to seek greater financial support from Britain.
- ○ It enabled Britain to further stretch the boundaries of its empire.

X   ○ The British Parliament refused consent for higher taxes.

This response is incorrect because the speaker talks about Britain's attempt to tax the American colonies without their consent, not about the British Parliament refusing consent for higher taxes.

✓   ◉ It led Britain to monitor more closely its colonial interests.

This response is correct. The speaker states that the Seven Years' War created a new sense of empire, which resulted in Britain's determination to govern its empire more closely, in other words, to monitor more closely its colonial interests.

X   ○ It caused the colonies to seek greater financial support from Britain.

This response is incorrect. The speaker states that the Seven Years' War intensified Britain's interest in things imperial. Whether the colonies sought financial support from Britain is not discussed.

X   ○ It enabled Britain to further stretch the boundaries of its empire.

This response is incorrect because this point is not addressed by the speaker.

Transcript

And then finally, briefly, ... [I want to] say a little bit about the way in which the Seven Years' War created a new sense of empire. [I have put a] question mark, [here] because there are questions about how new this [sense] is, but it certainly intensified Britain's interest in things imperial and, and I think most historians, both British and American, would agree that that new interest and that determination to govern the empire more closely played a key role in preparing the ground for the series of parliamentary attempts to tax the American colonies without their consent, which culminated in the rebellion and eventual independence of thirteen of them. So there's a close connection, and historians have always seen this, between the Seven Years' War and the American Revolution.

p. 153   # Select missing word

- ○ blood
- ● mood
- ○ damage
- ○ failure
- ○ heart

✗   ○ blood

This response is incorrect. Although the speaker mentions the fact that patients with heart failure have damaged hearts that are unable to pump blood effectively round the body, in the final part of the recording she refers to a psychological study of these patients. A psychological study would look at the mental well-being of the patients rather than their physical condition.

✓   ● mood

This response is correct. In the final part of the recording, the speaker refers to a psychological study of cardiac patients which was carried out to assess the link between heart failure and depression. Psychologists study depression by studying a patient's mood.

✗   ○ damage

This response is incorrect. Although the speaker mentions the phrase "damage to internal organs," this physical condition would not be the focus of a psychological study. Also, the meaning of the word "damage" by itself is too general to complete the final sentence. There is no evidence that the cardiac patients are psychologically "damaged."

✗   ○ failure

This response is incorrect. Although the speaker mentions the phrase "heart failure," this physical condition would not be the focus of a psychological study. Also, the meaning of the word "failure" by itself is too general to complete the final sentence. There is no evidence that the cardiac patients have "failed" in any psychological way.

✗   ○ heart

This response is incorrect. Although cardiac patients have problems with their heart, in the final part of the recording the speaker refers to a psychological study of these patients. A psychological study would look at the mental well-being of the patients rather than their physical condition.

When a patient has heart failure, their damaged heart isn't able to pump blood, and the oxygen that carries, effectively to the rest of the body. Symptoms of the condition, also known as congestive heart failure, range from swelling in the hands and feet to fatigue to damage to internal organs.

Close to half of patients diagnosed with heart failure will report being depressed, and of those people, about a third will experience serious depression. Now, it appears that having depression can make heart failure worse. Psychologist James Blumenthal, from Duke University in Durham, North Carolina, led a study in which researchers surveyed several hundred cardiac patients about their mood.

p. 157

Highlight incorrect words

So far in our discussion of chemical equations we have assumed that these reactions only go in one direction, the forward direction, from left to right as we read it in the equation. That's why our arrowhead points from left to right: reactants react together to make products. However, this is not exactly how things occur in reality. In fact, practically every chemical reaction is reversible, meaning the products can also react together to reform the reactants that they were made of. So instead of writing that single arrow facing from right to top, a more appropriate symbol would be a double arrow, one going from left to right and one going from right to left. Reactants are continually, continuously reacting to form produce. But at the same time as those products are formed, they remake the reactants. They're both going simultaneously, forming each other. This is what we would call a state of equality.

Transcript

So far in our discussion of chemical reactions we have assumed that these reactions only go in one direction, the forward direction, from left to right as we read it in the equation. That's why our arrow points from left to right: reactants react together to make products. However, this is not exactly how things occur in nature. In fact, practically every chemical reaction is reversible, meaning the products can also react together to reform the reactants that they were made of. So instead of writing that single arrow facing from left to right, a more appropriate symbol would be a double arrow, one going from left to right and one going from right to left. Reactants are continually, continuously reacting to form products. But at the same time as those products are formed, they remake the reactants. They're both going simultaneously, forming each other. This is what we would call a state of equilibrium.

p. 162

Write from dictation

These arguments are accepted by most researchers in the field.

Transcript

These arguments are accepted by most researchers in the field.

Glossary

abstract (adj.)	relating to ideas rather than things; the opposite of concrete
abstract (n.)	summary of an academic text or document
audio progress indicator	bar within the audio status box showing the elapsed time of the audio
audio status box	box controlling audio functions for item types with audio recordings
authentic	taken from real situations
automated scoring system	computer-based speech recognition and essay-scoring engines
beep	sound used to indicate the missing word(s) in the item type *Select missing word*
biometrics	measurement of physical or behavioral characteristics as a means of verifying personal identity
blanks	gaps in text
blue box	word bank in the item type *Reading: Fill in the blanks*
breach	an action that breaks a rule, or agreement
checkbox	box featured next to a response option for selecting more than one response option as in the item type *Multiple-choice, choose multiple answers*; the response option can be selected or deselected by clicking on the checkbox.
checkmark	symbol used inside a checkbox or radio button to show that the response option has been selected
cliché	overused expression or idea that has lost its impact
coherence	logic, or overall sense of being clear and easy to understand
colloquialism	informal expression often used in conversation
communicative skills	key language skills required to interact in social situations: listening, reading, speaking, writing
concordance	agreement with
concrete (adj.)	relating to real or actual things
connotation	the implied meaning of a word or expression; the meanings associated with a word

denotation	the direct or actual meaning of a word or expression
deselect	undo or remove a selection made in a checkbox or radio button
discourse	written or spoken communication
discourse marker	a word or phrase used to organize or fulfil a function within written or spoken language. For example, "anyway" is a discourse marker to change topic.
drop down arrow	clickable button positioned to the right of a blank in the item type *Reading & writing: Fill in the blanks*, used to display the drop down list
drop down list	list that displays in the blanks of the item type *Reading & writing: Fill in the blanks*
enabling skills	skills contributing to communicative ability: grammar, oral fluency, pronunciation, spelling, vocabulary, written discourse
Erasable Noteboard Booklet	writing surface provided for note taking
exchange	the act of giving and receiving information in communication
explicit	clearly and fully expressed
false starts	occasions when a speaker stops in the middle of speaking to reformulate the message and then starts again
headset	headphones and microphone
hesitation	pause or unsteadiness in speech
idiom	expression with a meaning that differs from the meaning of the actual words
image	visual input for the item type *Describe image*
implicit	implied rather than expressed; the opposite of explicit
increment	the amount by which a number, value or amount increases
infringe	break or exceed the limits of
integrated skills item type	item type that assesses more than one skill, for example, listening and speaking, reading and writing
item	task in the test consisting of instructions, question or prompt, answer opportunities, and scoring rules

item type	form of an item defined by the presentation, the nature of the task, the skills addressed and the scoring rules
lecture	talk or presentation
long-answer item type	item type that requires an extended response
"Next" button	button on the test screen that allows you to move to the next screen
non-verbal	not involving words
palm vein scans	a means of verifying identity using technology that recognizes palm vein patterns
partial credit	score on an item that is more than zero but less than the maximum score points available for the item
passage	text
pen	writing tool provided for note taking on an Erasable Noteboard Booklet
prompt	stimulus to an item or a task
radio button	button featured next to a response option for selecting a single response option as in the item type *Multiple-choice, choose single answer*; the response option can be selected or deselected by clicking on the radio button
register	the style of language used to communicate in particular contexts for specific purposes
response	answer
response box	typing area for item types that require written responses
response option	answer choice
score (v.)	assign points to responses
score (n.)	points assigned to responses
select text	choose text in the response box
short-answer item type	item type that requires a brief (one word or phrase) response
synonym	word with the same meaning, or similar meaning, as another word

test administrator	a member of staff at a test center
test delivery workstation or workstation	computer terminal used to take PTE Academic
test taker	examinee, candidate
testing room	place where PTE Academic is taken
timer	clock featured on screen that counts down the remaining time
tone	sound used to indicate the end of preparation time for some speaking item types
topic sentence	sentence that explains what a paragraph or passage is about
transcript	written copy of audio material
turn-taking	the convention that people follow in oral communication, in which participants respond or volunteer information one by one
utterance	speech that people produce for oral communication
verbal	involving spoken words

Appendix CEF language descriptors

The Common European Framework of Reference for Languages (CEF or CEFR; Council of Europe, 2001) is a widely accepted standard of ability or performance in language testing and contains scales that describe a series of levels of language proficiency. According to the CEF, there are six levels.

Proficient User: C1 (Effective Operational Proficiency); C2 (Mastery)
Independent User: B1 (Threshold); B2 (Vantage)
Basic User: A1 (Breakthrough); A2 (Waystage)

"1" and "2" indicate respectively lower and higher levels of ability within the broad bands A (Basic), B (Independent) and C (Proficient).

Common Reference Levels: global scale

Proficient User	C2	Can understand with ease virtually everything heard or read. Can summarise information from different spoken and written sources, reconstructing arguments and accounts in a coherent presentation. Can express him/herself spontaneously, very fluently and precisely, differentiating finer shades of meaning even in more complex situations.
	C1	Can understand a wide range of demanding, longer texts, and recognise implicit meaning. Can express him/herself fluently and spontaneously without much obvious searching for expressions. Can use language flexibly and effectively for social, academic and professional purposes. Can produce clear, well-structured, detailed text on complex subjects, showing controlled use of organisational patterns, connectors and cohesive devices.
Independent User	B2	Can understand the main ideas of complex text on both concrete and abstract topics, including technical discussions in his/her field of specialisation. Can interact with a degree of fluency and spontaneity that makes regular interaction with native speakers quite possible without strain for either party. Can produce clear, detailed text on a wide range of subjects and explain a viewpoint on a topical issue giving the advantages and disadvantages of various options.
	B1	Can understand the main points of clear standard input on familiar matters regularly encountered in work, school, leisure, etc. Can deal with most situations likely to arise whilst travelling in an area where the language is spoken. Can produce simple connected text on topics which are familiar or of personal interest. Can describe experiences and events, dreams, hopes and ambitions and briefly give reasons and explanations for opinions and plans.
Basic User	A2	Can understand sentences and frequently used expressions related to areas of most immediate relevance (e.g. very basic personal and family information, shopping, local geography, employment). Can communicate in simple and routine tasks requiring a simple and direct exchange of information on familiar and routine matters. Can describe in simple terms aspects of his/her background, immediate environment and matters in areas of immediate need.
	A1	Can understand and use familiar everyday expressions and very basic phrases aimed at the satisfaction of needs of a concrete type. Can introduce him/herself and others and can ask and answer questions about personal details such as where he/she lives, people he/she knows and things he/she has. Can interact in a simple way provided the other person talks slowly and clearly and is prepared to help.

Common Reference Levels: self-assessment grid

		A1	A2	B1
UNDERSTANDING	**Listening**	I can recognise familiar words and very basic phrases concerning myself, my family and immediate concrete surroundings when people speak slowly and clearly.	I can understand phrases and the highest frequency vocabulary related to areas of most immediate personal relevance (e.g. very basic personal and family information, shopping, local area, employment). I can catch the main point in short, clear, simple messages and announcements.	I can understand the main points of clear standard speech on familiar matters regularly encountered in work, school, leisure, etc. I can understand the main point of many radio or TV programmes on current affairs or topics of personal or professional interest when the delivery is relatively slow and clear.
	Reading	I can understand familiar names, words and very simple sentences, for example on notices and posters or in catalogues.	I can read very short, simple texts. I can find specific, predictable information in simple everyday material such as advertisements, prospectuses, menus and timetables and I can understand short simple personal letters.	I can understand texts that consist mainly of high frequency everyday or job-related language. I can understand the description of events, feelings and wishes in personal letters.
SPEAKING	**Spoken Interaction**	I can interact in a simple way provided the other person is prepared to repeat or rephrase things at a slower rate of speech and help me formulate what I'm trying to say. I can ask and answer simple questions in areas of the immediate need or on very familiar topics.	I can communicate in simple and routine tasks requiring a simple and direct exchange of information on familiar topics and activities. I can handle very short social exchanges, even though I can't usually understand enough to keep the conversation going myself.	I can deal with most situations likely to arise whilst travelling in an area where the language is spoken. I can enter unprepared into conversation on topics that are familiar, of personal interest or pertinent to everyday life (e.g. family, hobbies, work, travel and current events).
	Spoken Production	I can use simple phrases and sentences to describe where I live and people I know.	I can use a series of phrases and sentences to describe in simple terms my family and other people, living conditions, my educational background and my present or most recent job.	I can connect phrases in a simple way in order to describe experiences and events, my dreams, hopes and ambitions. I can briefly give reasons and explanations for opinions and plans. I can narrate a story or relate the plot of a book or film and describe my reactions.
WRITING	**Writing**	I can write a short, simple postcard, for example sending holiday greetings. I can fill in forms with personal details, for example entering my name, nationality and address on a hotel registration form.	I can write short, simple notes and messages relating to matters in areas of immediate need. I can write a very simple personal letter, for example thanking someone for something.	I can write simple connected text on topics which are familiar or of personal interest. I can write personal letters describing experiences and impressions.

B2	C1	C2
I can understand extended speech and lectures and follow even complex lines of argument provided the topic is reasonably familiar. I can understand most TV news and current affairs programmes. I can understand the majority of films in standard dialect.	I can understand extended speech even when it is not clearly structured and when relationships are only implied and not signalled explicitly. I can understand television programmes and films without too much effort.	I have no difficulty in understanding any kind of spoken language, whether live or broadcast, even when delivered at fast native speed, provided I have some time to get familiar with the accent.
I can read articles and reports concerned with contemporary problems in which the writers adopt particular attitudes or viewpoints. I can understand contemporary literary prose.	I can understand long and complex factual and literary texts, appreciating distinctions of style. I can understand specialised articles and longer technical instructions, even when they do not relate to my field.	I can read with ease virtually all forms of the written language, including abstract, structurally or linguistically complex texts such as manuals, specialised articles and literary works.
I can interact with a degree of fluency and spontaneity that makes regular interaction with native speakers quite possible. I can take an active part in discussion in familiar contexts, accounting for and sustaining my views.	I can express myself fluently and spontaneously without much obvious searching for expressions. I can use language flexibly and effectively for social and professional purposes. I can formulate ideas and opinions with precision and relate my contribution skifully to those of other speakers.	I can take part effortlessly in any conversation or discussion and have a good familiarity with idiomatic expressions and colloquialisms. I can express myself fluently and convey finer shades of meaning precisely. If I do have a problem I can backtrack and restructure around the difficulty so smoothly that other people are hardly aware of it.
I can present clear, detailed descriptions on a wide range of subjects related to my field of interest. I can explain a viewpoint on a topical issue giving the advantages and disadvantages of various options.	I can present clear, detailed description of complex subjects integrating sub-themes, developing particular points and rounding off with an appropriate conclusion.	I can present a clear, smoothly flowing description or argument in a style appropriate to the context and with an effective logical structure which helps the recipient to notice and remember significant points.
I can write clear, detailed text on a wide range of subjects related to my interests. I can write an essay or report, passing on information or giving reasons in support of or against a particular point of view. I can write letters highlighting the personal significance of events and experiences.	I can express myself in clear, well-structured text, expressing points of view at some length. I can write about complex subjects in a letter, an essay or a report, underlining what I consider to be the salient issues. I can select style apoporiate to the reader in mind.	I can write clear, smoothly flowing text in an appropriate style. I can write complex letters, reports or articles which present a case with an effective logical structure which helps the recipient to notice and remember significant points. I can write summaries and reviews of professional or literary works.

Common Reference Levels: qualitative aspects of spoken language use

	RANGE	ACCURACY	FLUENCY
C2	Shows great flexibility reformulating ideas in differing linguistic forms to convey finer shades of meaning precisely, to give emphasis, to differentiate and to eliminate ambiguity. Also has a good command of idiomatic expressions and colloquialisms.	Maintains consistent grammatical control of complex language, even while attention is otherwise engaged (e.g. in forward planning, in monitoring others' reactions).	Can express him/herself spontaneously at length with a natural colloquial flow, avoiding or backtracking around any difficulty so smoothly that the interlocutor is hardly aware of it.
C1	Has a good command of a broad range of language allowing him/her to select a formulation to express him/herself clearly in an appropriate style on a wide range of general, academic, professional or leisure topics without having to restrict what he/she wants to say.	Consistently maintains a high degree of grammatical accuracy; errors are rare, difficult to spot and generally corrected when they do occur.	Can express him/herself fluently and spontaneously, almost effortlessly. Only a conceptually difficult subject can hinder a natural, smooth flow of language.
B2+			
B2	Has a sufficient range of language to be able to give clear descriptions, express viewpoints on most general topics, without much conspicuous searching for words, using some complex sentence forms to do so.	Shows a relatively high degree of grammatical control. Does not make errors which cause misunderstanding, and can correct most of his/her mistakes.	Can produce stretches of language with a fairly even tempo; although he/she can be hesitant as he/she searches for patterns and expressions. There are few noticeably long pauses.
B1+			
B1	Has enough language to get by, with sufficient vocabulary to express him/herself with some hesitation and circumlocutions on topics such as family, hobbies and interests, work, travel, and current events.	Uses reasonably accurately a repertoire of frequently used 'routines' and patterns associated with more predictable situations.	Can keep going comprehensibly, even though pausing for grammatical and lexical planning and repair is very evident, especially in longer stretches of free production.
A2+			
A2	Uses basic sentence patterns with memorised phrases, groups of a few words and formulae in order to communicate limited information in simple everyday situations.	Uses some simple structures correctly, but still systematically makes basic mistakes.	Can make him/herself understood in very short utterances, even though pauses, false starts and reformulation are very evident.
A1	Has a very basic repertoire of words and simple phrases related to personal details and particular concrete situations.	Shows only limited control of a few simple grammatical structures and sentence patterns in a memorised repertoire.	Can manage very short, isolated, mainly pre-packaged utterances, with much pausing to search for expressions, to articulate less familiar words, and to repair communication.

© Council of Europe

INTERACTION	COHERENCE
Can interact with ease and skill, picking up and using non-verbal and intonational cues apparently effortlessly. Can interweave his/her contribution into the joint discourse with fully natural turntaking, referencing, allusion making, etc.	Can create coherent and cohesive discourse making full and appropriate use of a variety of organisational patterns and a wide range of connectors and other cohesive devices.
Can select a suitable phrase from a readily available range of discourse functions to preface his remarks in order to get or to keep the floor and to relate his/her own contributions skilfully to those of other speakers.	Can produce clear, smoothly flowing, well-structured speech, showing controlled use of organisational patterns, connectors and cohesive devices.
Can initiate discourse, take his/her turn when appropriate and end conversation when he/she needs to, though he/she may not always do this elegantly. Can help the discussion along on familiar ground confirming comprehension, inviting others in, etc.	Can use a limited number of cohesive devices to link his/her utterances into clear, coherent discourse, though there may be some 'jumpiness' in a long contribution.
Can initiate, maintain and close simple face-to-face conversation on topics that are familiar or of personal interest. Can repeat back part of what someone has said to confirm mutual understanding.	Can link a series of shorter, discrete simple elements into a connected, linear sequence of points.
Can answer questions and respond to simple statements. Can indicate when he/she is following but is rarely able to understand enough to keep conversation going of his/her own accord.	Can link groups of words with simple connectors like 'but' and 'because'.
Can ask and answer questions about personal details. Can interact in a simple way but communication is totally dependent on repetition, rephrasing and repair.	Can link words or groups of words with very basic linear connectors like 'and' or 'then'.

Overall listening comprehension

	OVERALL LISTENING COMPREHENSION
C2	Has no difficulty in understanding any kind of spoken language, whether live or broadcast, delivered at fast native speed.
C1	Can understand enough to follow extended speech on abstract and complex topics beyond his/her own field, though he/she may need to confirm occasional details, especially if the accent is unfamiliar. Can recognise a wide range of idiomatic expressions and colloquialisms, appreciating register shifts. Can follow extended speech even when it is not clearly structured and when relationships are only implied and not signalled explicitly.
B2	Can understand standard spoken language, live or broadcast, on both familiar and unfamiliar topics normally encountered in personal, social, academic or vocational life. Only extreme background noise, inadequate discourse structure and/or idiomatic usage influences the ability to understand.
B2	Can understand the main ideas of propositionally and linguistically complex speech on both concrete and abstract topics delivered in a standard dialect, including technical discussions in his/her field of specialisation. Can follow extended speech and complex lines of argument provided the topic is reasonably familiar, and the direction of the talk is sign-posted by explicit markers.
B1	Can understand straightforward factual information about common everyday or job-related topics, identifying both general messages and specific details, provided speech is clearly articulated in a generally familiar accent.
B1	Can understand the main points of clear standard speech on familiar matters regularly encountered in work, school, leisure etc., including short narratives.
A2	Can understand enough to be able to meet needs of a concrete type provided speech is clearly and slowly articulated.
A2	Can understand phrases and expressions related to areas of most immediate priority (e.g. very basic personal and family information, shopping, local geography, employment) provided speech is clearly and slowly articulated.
A1	Can follow speech which is very slow and carefully articulated, with long pauses for him/her to assimilate meaning.

© Council of Europe

Overall reading comprehension

	OVERALL READING COMPREHENSION
C2	Can understand and interpret critically virtually all forms of the written language including abstract, structurally complex, or highly colloquial literary and non-literary writings. Can understand a wide range of long and complex texts, appreciating subtle distinctions of style and implicit as well as explicit meaning.
C1	Can understand in detail lengthy, complex texts, whether or not they relate to his/her own area of speciality, provided he/she can reread difficult sections.
B2	Can read with a large degree of independence, adapting style and speed of reading to different texts and purposes, and using appropriate reference sources selectively. Has a broad active reading vocabulary, but may experience some difficulty with low frequency idioms.
B1	Can read straightforward factual texts on subjects related to his/her field and interest with a satisfactory level of comprehension.
A2	Can understand short, simple texts on familiar matters of a concrete type which consist of high frequency everyday or job-related language.
A2	Can understand short, simple texts containing the highest frequency vocabulary, including a proportion of shared international vocabulary items.
A1	Can understand very short, simple texts a single phrase at a time, picking up familiar names, words and basic phrases and rereading as required.

© Council of Europe

Overall oral production

	OVERALL ORAL PRODUCTION
C2	Can produce clear, smoothly flowing well-structured speech with an effective logical structure which helps the recipient to notice and remember significant points.
C1	Can give clear, detailed descriptions and presentations on complex subjects, integrating sub-themes, developing particular points and rounding off with an appropriate conclusion.
B2	Can give clear, systematically developed descriptions and presentations, with appropriate highlighting of significant points, and relevant supporting detail.
B2	Can give clear, detailed descriptions and presentations on a wide range of subjects related to his/her field of interest, expanding and supporting ideas with subsidiary points and relevant examples.
B1	Can reasonably fluently sustain a straightforward description of one of a variety of subjects within his/her field of interest, presenting it as a linear sequence of points.
A2	Can give a simple description or presentation of people, living or working conditions, daily routines, likes/dislikes, etc. as a short series of simple phrases and sentences linked into a list.
A1	Can produce simple mainly isolated phrases about people and places.

© Council of Europe

Overall written production

	OVERALL WRITTEN PRODUCTION
C2	Can write clear, smoothly flowing, complex texts in an appropriate and effective style and a logical structure which helps the reader to find significant points.
C1	Can write clear, well-structured texts of complex subjects, underlining the relevant salient issues, expanding and supporting points of view at some length with subsidiary points, reasons and relevant examples, and rounding off with an appropriate conclusion.
B2	Can write clear, detailed texts on a variety of subjects related to his/her field of interest, synthesising and evaluating information and arguments from a number of sources.
B1	Can write straightforward connected texts on a range of familiar subjects within his/her field of interest, by linking a series of shorter discrete elements into a linear sequence.
A2	Can write a series of simple phrases and sentences linked with simple connectors like 'and', 'but' and 'because'.
A1	Can write simple isolated phrases and sentences.

© Council of Europe

Acknowledgements

For permission to use copyrighted materials in the *Official Guide*, we would like to thank the following:

Using SPSS for Windows and Macintosh Analyzing and Understanding Data by Samuel Green and Neil Salkind, International Edition, 5th edition, 2007. Reproduced by permission of Pearson Education, Inc. (pp. 40, 41); *How we are: Photographing Britain from the 1840s to the Present* by Val Williams and Susan Bright, Tate Publishing, 2007. Reproduced by permission of Tate Trustees (p. 44); Graph on job satisfaction, reproduced with permission of Reed Business Information, from INDUSTRIAL DISTRIBUTION.ONLINE, 2007; permission conveyed through Copyright Clearance Center, Inc. (pp. 50, 51); *Population Growth in More, Less Developed Countries.* Courtesy of Population Reference Bureau (p. 54); *The Big Issues Women's Rights in Development: Building women's rights to achieve sustainable economies and livelihoods* by Ann Killen, Copyright © 2009 the University of South Australia and Ann Killen (pp. 55, 56, 167); *50 Years Since Sputnik* by Piers Bizony, University of Bath Lecture Podcast. Courtesy of Piers Bizony (pp. 60, 177); Courtesy of S-cool Limited (pp. 73, 74); Miller/Benjamin/North, ECONOMICS PUBLIC ISSUES, © 2008, 2005, 2003, 2001 Pearson Education, Inc. Reproduced by permission of Pearson Education, Inc. (p. 77); Courtesy of voanews.com (pp. 91, 92); *Voyages of Discovery* by Lynne Withey, reprinted by permission of HarperCollins Publishers, and by the permission of Russell & Volkening as agents for the author. Copyright © 1987 by Lynne Withey (p. 95); *Learning Opportunities for All: Pedagogy in multigrade and monograde classrooms in the Turks and Caicos Islands* by Chris Berry from *Education for All and Multigrade Teaching*, edited by Angela W. Little, 1st edition, 2006, with kind permission from Springer Science and Business Media (pp. 96, 97); *In Search of Inland Treasures* by Belinda Archer, © The Financial Times (pp. 100); *50 Psychology Classics*, published by Nicholas Brealey Publishing 2007 (pp. 105, 183); Courtesy of Laureate Education Inc. (pp. 106, 107, 169); *Living online: This is your space* © New Scientist (pp. 109, 184); Reproduced by kind permission of Aon Limited (pp. 108, 109, 167); *Museum and Society* published by University of Leicester, Department of Museum Studies, Volume 5, Issue 2, Jul 2007 Title: *Authentic recreation: living history and leisure.* Author: Lain Hart http://www.le.ac.uk/ms/m&s/Issue%2014/lainhart.pdf (pp. 113, 114, 184, 185); 2006 Boyer Lectures, *Lecture 1: The Golden Age* by Ian Macfarlane, first broadcast by Radio National, 12 November 2006, reproduced by permission of the Australian Broadcasting Corporation and ABC Online. © 2006 ABC. All rights reserved (pp. 125, 169, 170); Excerpt from the interview *View from the Top: Bob Iger* © The Financial Times (pp. 128, 186); *It's not news, it's fark* by Drew Curtis, Penguin website interview podcast, published by Penguin Group (USA) (pp. 131, 170); University of Virginia Lecture Podcasts: Charlottesville Albemarle Democratic Party Breakfast Series: *Are election machines vulnerable?* Courtesy of Jim Heilman (pp. 134, 187); Reprinted with permission from Knowledge@Wharton http://knowledge.wharton.upenn.edu (pp. 135, 136, 141, 172); *Biological Bases of Mind and Behavior 1.* Courtesy of John F. Kihlstrom (pp. 138, 139, 188); Excerpt from lecture by Donald R. Sadoway, Professor of Materials Chemistry in the Department of Materials Science and Engineering at the Massachusetts Institute of Technology, http://ocw.mit.edu/OcwWeb/Materials-Science-and-Engineering/3-091Fall-2004/LectureNotes/index.htm (pp. 144, 189); *Propaganda and Control of the Public Mind* by Noam Chomsky, AK Press, 1998 (pp. 146, 170); Excerpt from the lecture *Britain and the Seven Years War* by Eliga Gould, an associate professor of history at the University of New Hampshire, author of a book about the American Revolution and the "pacification" of the Atlantic world (pp. 149, 190); *Simulating the Look and Feel of Surgery* by Nikolas Blevins, Kenneth Salisbury, 2007, Stanford University (pp. 151, 173); VOA American Life *Research Shows Being Depressed Hurts Ailing Hearts* by Rose Holbin and Chapel Hill, Voice of America (pp. 153, 192); PBS Nova: WGBH Science Unit Podcast, 2007, from NOVA/WGBH Educational Foundation Copyright © 2007 WGBH/Boston (pp. 154, 155, 173); Excerpt from *Sensible Chemistry Lectures.* Courtesy of Bruce McHam (pp. 157, 158, 192); From *Mistress of the Art of Death* by Ariana Franklin, Copyright © Ariana Franklin, 2007. Reprinted by permission of Penguin Group (Canada), a Division of Pearson Canada Inc., and Penguin Group (USA) Inc. (pp. 160, 1173); CEF language descriptors © Council of Europe (pp. 197–204)

For permission to use copyrighted materials on the CD-ROM, we would like to thank the following:

Practice set 1, Speaking items

© Pearson Australia: *E tips for A Grades: Tackling the College paper* (items 1 and 2) and *Have no career fear* published by Pearson Higher Education (item 3)

Information Please® Database, © 2007 Pearson Education, Inc.: *Botswana* (item 4); *Valentine's Day History: Pagan festivals, Christian saints, Chaucer's love birds, and the Greeting Card Association of America* by Borgna Brunner (item 5); *The Rise and Fall of Roller Coasters: From the Russian countryside to Disneyland* by Marcus McGraw (item 6); *Atlantis Myth or history?* by Holly Hartman (item 7); *The History of Skyscrapers: A race to the top* by Karen Barss (item 21, image); *Wonder Women: Profiles of leading female CEOs and business executives* by John Gettings, David Johnson, Borgna Brunner, and Chris Frantz (item 28); *Daylight Saving Time: A trip around the world reveals that time isn't a synchronized science* by John Gettings and Borgna Brunner (item 29)

United Nations Development Program, Human Development Report 2006, United Nations Development Program. Reproduced with permission of Palgrave Macmillan (item 27)

Practice set 1, Writing items

Information Please® Database, © 2007 Pearson Education, Inc.: *Dowries: The joining of money and marriage* by David Johnson (item 1)

Practice set 1, Reading items

Sioux from *The Columbia Encyclopedia*, 6th edition, edited by Paul Lagasse © 2007 Columbia University Press. Reprinted with the permission of the publisher (item 1)

Information Please® Database, © 2007 Pearson Education, Inc.: *Over Six Billion Counted World Population Reaches New Milestone* by Borgna Brunner (item 2); *What's the Symbolism of the Irish Flag? History and symbolism of the Irish tricolour* by Borgna Brunner (item 3); *Botswana* (items 4 and 7); *Who's Who in Afghanistan: A look at some of the key players: Muhammad Daoud* by David Johnson (item 5); *Valentine's Day History: Pagan festivals, Christian saints, Chaucer's love birds, and the Greeting Card Association of America* by Borgna Brunner (item 6); *New Year's Traditions: Auld Lang Syne and other New Year's customs* by Borgna Brunner (item 8); *What is Haute Couture? Uncovering the business of high fashion* by David Johnson (item 9); *The Ides of March: Just one of a dozen Ides that occur every month of the year* by Borgna Brunner (item 10); *Measuring Mountains: The world's highest peak and past pretenders to the throne* by Borgna Brunner (item 11); *Fun Facts About Skyscrapers: From the father of the skyscraper to a building with a view* by Karen Barss (item 12); *Why Spanish Accents Can Be So Different: Accents speak to variety of Hispanic world* by David Johnson (item 14); *The History of Skyscrapers: A race to the top* by Karen Barss (item 15); *C. S. Lewis: The Creator of Narnia–Biography* by Ann-Marie Imbornoni (item 16)

Practice set 1, Listening items

Information Please® Database, © 2007 Pearson Education, Inc.: *The History of Skyscrapers: A race to the top* by Karen Barss (item 4); *What Is Feng Shui? The classical Chinese system for seeking harmony* by David Johnson (item 12); *Atlantis: Myth or history?* by Holly Hartman (item 13); *C. S. Lewis: The Creator of Narnia–Biography* by Ann-Marie Imbornoni (item 14); *Why Spanish Accents Can Be So Different: Accents speak to variety of Hispanic world* by David Johnson (item 16); *Joseph Heller Remembered* by Ricco Villanueva Siasoco (item 17)

Practice set 2, Speaking items

Cotton: The Biography of a Revolutionary Fiber by Stephen Yafa, Penguin Group (USA), 2006 (item 1); *Museum: Behind the Scenes at the Metropolitan Museum of Art* by Danny Danziger, Penguin Group (USA), 2008 (item 2); *How Language Works: How Babies Babble, Words Change Meaning and Languages Live or Die* by David Crystal (Penguin Books, 2005). Copyright © David Crystal 2005. Reproduced by permission of Penguin Books Ltd. (item 3); *My China* by Kwong Kylie. Published by Lantern, Penguin Group (Australia), 2007 (item 4); *Ego & Soul: The Modern West in Search of Meaning* by Carroll John. Published by Scribe Publications, 2008 (item 5)

Information Please® Database, © 2007 Pearson Education, Inc.: *World's Most Populous Urban Agglomerations: 2005* (item 21) and *World's Most Expensive Cities 2008* (item 22)

Australian Share Price Index 20 December 2008 © 2009 Standard & Poor's, a Division of The McGraw-Hill Companies, Inc (S&P) and ASX Limited ABN 98 008 624 691 (ASX) 2009. All rights reserved. This material is reproduced with the permission of ASX and S&P. This material should not be reproduced, stored in a retrieval system or transmitted in any form whether in whole or in part without the prior written permission of ASX and S&P (item 23); KidsHealth (item 27); *Energy & Enviro Finland* from http://www.energy-enviro.fi/index.php?PAGE=160&LANG=1&COMPANY=enviro (item 28)

Practice set 2, Writing items

Information Please® Database, © 2007 Pearson Education, Inc.: *Dangers of Deflation Defined* (item 1); *The History of the Internet: From a simple 300-mile transmission to a global network in cyberspace* by Ricco Villanueva Siasoco (item 2); *The Wage Gap: A History of Pay Inequity and the Equal Pay Act* by Borgna Brunner (item 3)

Practice set 2, Reading items

The Columbia Encyclopedia, 6th edition, edited by Paul Lagasse © 2007 Columbia University Press. Reprinted with the permission of the publisher: *Excise Taxes* (item 1); *Angkor* (item 2); *X-ray crystallography* (item 4); *Open Door Policy* (item 7)

Information Please® Database, © 2007 Pearson Education, Inc.: *The Curious History of the Gregorian Calendar: Eleven days that never were* by Ben Snowden (item 3); *Modern Olympic Games* (item 6); *The Biggest One-Day Declines in the Dow Jones Industrial Average: Economic and political turmoil often result in wild swings of stock prices* by Beth Rowen (item 8); *Gap Between Rich and Poor: World Income Inequality in 2002 Percentage share of income (poorest and richest 20% of population)* (item 9); *2004 Olympics: Athens* (item 10); *A Weighty Discovery in Particle Physics* (item 14)

© Pearson Australia: *Basic Personal Counselling: A Training Manual for Counsellors*, 5th edition by David Geldard and Kathyrn Geldard (item 11); *Event Management Instructor's Manual*, 3rd edition by Van Der Wagen (item 12); *The Australian Legal System: History, Institutions and Method* by Russell Hinchy, The University of Queensland 2007 (item 13)

Ernest Shackleton Explorer from Who2.com (item 15)

Practice set 2, Listening items

© Pearson Australia: *Introduction To Tourism: Development Issues and Changes* 5th edition by Colin Michael Hall, University of Canterbury (item 1); *Psychology And Life: Australasian* edition by Richard Gerrig, Stony Brook University, Philip Zimbardo, Stanford University, Andrew Campbell, University of Sydney, Steven Cumming, University of Sydney, Fiona J. Wilkes, University of Western Sydney, published in 2008 (item 3); *E tips for A Grades: Free Money* (item 14)

James Cook from *The Columbia Encyclopedia*, 6th edition, edited by Paul Lagasse © 2007 Columbia University Press. Reprinted with the permission of the publisher (item 4)

Sea of Dangers by Blainey Geoffrey. Published by Viking, Penguin Group (Australia), 2008 (item 5); *The Lot: In Words* by Leunig Michael. Published by Viking, Penguin Group (Australia), 2008 (item 9); *Fire* by Manfield Christine. Published by Lantern, Penguin Group (Australia), 2008 (item 10); *Outback Pioneers* by McHugh Evan. Published by Viking, Penguin Group (Australia), 2008 (item 16)

Penguin Group (USA) Inc.: *The Rough Guide to the Internet* by Peter Buckley (item 6); *Dealing with Darwin: How Great Companies Innovate at Every Phase of Their Evolution* by Geoffrey A. Moore. Published by Penguin, 2005 (item 8); *Generation Debt* by Anya Kamenetz. Published by Penguin, 2006 (item 11); *The Green Year: 365 Small Things You Can Do to Make a Big Difference* by Jodi Helmer (item 12); *The World's Banker: A Story of Failed States, Financial Crises, and the Wealth and Poverty of Nations* by Sebastian Mallaby. Published by Penguin, 2006 (item 15)

Reproduced by permission of Penguin Books Ltd.: *Lives of The Artists* Vol. 1 by Giorgio Vasari, translated by George Bull (Penguin Classics, 1987). Copyright © George Bull, 1965 (item 7); *The Pleasures and Sorrows of Work* by Alain de Botton (Penguin Books, 2009). Copyright © Alain de Botton, 2009 (item 13)

Practice set 3, Speaking items

The Content Makers by Margaret Simons, published by Penguin, Penguin Group (Australia), 2007 (item 1); *The Future of the Internet* by Jonathan Zittrain (Penguin Books, 2008, 2009). Copyright © Jonathan Zittrain, 2008. Reproduced by permission of Penguin Books Ltd. (item 2); *The Complete Idiot's Guide to Journalism* by Passante Christopher K. Published by Alpha, Penguin Group (USA), 2007 (item 3); *Dispatches for the New York Tribune: Selected Journalism of Karl Marx* by Karl Marx and edited by James Ledbetter (Penguin Books, 2007). Selection and editorial matter copyright © James Ledbetter, 2007. Reproduced by permission of Penguin Books Ltd. (item 4); *The Decisive Moment: How the Brain Makes Up Its Mind* by Lehrer Jonah. Published by Text, Text Publishing, 2009, Canongate Books (item 5); *The Well Dressed Ape* by Holmes Hannah, published by Scribe Publications, 2009 (item 7)

© Dorling Kindersley: *Australia: World Rankings* (item 21); *Brazil: Climate* (item 22); *China: Economics* (item 23); *Ecuador: Tourism* (item 24); *Finland: Politics* (item 25); *New Zealand: Economics* (item 26)

Open University iTunes © Copyright The Open University: *Free Speech* from Album *Ethics Bites* by Tim Scalon (item 27); *Fungi Academic Commentary* from Album *Biology Uniformity and Diversity* by David Robinson (item 28); *Being a scientist* from Album *Challenge of the Social Sciences* (item 29)

Practice set 3, Writing items

The Reading Bug ... & How You Can Help Your Child to Catch it by Paul Jennings. Published by Penguin, Penguin Group (Australia), 2003 (item 1); *A Short History of the Twentieth Century* by Geoffrey Blainey. Published by Penguin, Penguin Group (Australia), 2007 (item 3)

Practice set 3, Reading items

Australia: Education © Dorling Kindersley (item 1); *Endangered: Tasmania's Wild Places*, extract from Preface by Martin Hawes. Published by Viking, Penguin Group (Australia), 2007 (item 2); *A Century of Colour Photography* by Pamela Roberts. Published by Viking, Penguin Group (Australia), and Carlton Books, 2007 (item 4); *The Well Dressed Ape* by Holmes Hannah. Published by Scribe Publications, 2009 (item 6); *Boringology: 50 of the most unglamorous scientific projects that are changing the world* by Dobson Roger. Published by Marshall Cavendish, Marshall Cavendish U 2009 (item 7); *Sex Sleep Eat Drink Dream: A Day in the Life of Your Body* by Ackerman Jennifer. Published by Scribe Publications, 2008 (item 8); *Small Wonders: How Microbes Rule Our World* by Ben-Barak Idan. Published by Scribe Publications, 2008 (item 11); *Fire* by Manfield Christine. Published by Lantern, Penguin Group (Australia), 2008 (item 12); Extract for *Finnikin of the Rock* by Melina Marchetta. Published by Penguin Group (Australia) (item 13); *An Exacting Heart: The Story of Hephzibah Menuhin* by Jacqueline Kent. Published by Viking, Penguin Group (Australia), 2008 (item 14); *Bright from the Start: The Simple Way to Nurture Your Child's Developing Mind* by Dr Jill Stamm with Paula Spencer. Published by Viking, Penguin Group (Australia), 2007 (item 17)

Reproduced by permission of Penguin Books Ltd.: *Freakonomics* by Steven Levitt & Steven J Dubner (Allen Lane, The Penguin Press 2005). Copyright © Steven Levitt & Steven J Dubner, 2005 (item 3); *Eat Your Heart Out* by Felicity Lawrence (Penguin Books 2008). Copyright © Felicity Lawrence, 2008 (item 5); *The Fabric of the Cosmos* by Brian Greene (Penguin Books 2004, 2007). Copyright © Brian Greene, 2004 (items 9 and 10); *The Age of Turbulence* by Alan Greenspan (Penguin Books, 2007, 2008). Copyright © Alan Greenspan, 2007 (item 15); *Blink* by Malcolm Gladwell (Allen Lane 2005). Copyright © Malcolm Gladwell, 2005. By permission of Little, Brown & Company (item 16)

Practice set 3, Listening items

Open University iTunes © Copyright The Open University: *Injustice and Inequality* from Album *Earth in Crises: Environmental Consequences* (item 1); *Archaeology: Origins of Agriculture* from Album *World Archeology* (item 2); *Consciousness: the central psychological question* from Album *Cognitive Psychology* (items 3 and 7); *What DU311 offers* from Album *Earth in crisis: environmental policy in an international context* (item 4); *It's Elementary: A Chemist's View* from Album *Takeaway Science* (item 5); *Approaches to genre* from Album *Start writing fiction* by Patricia Duncker (item 6); *Computers and Processors Academic Commentary* from Album *Computers and Processors* by Bernie Clark (item 8); *Developing the Idea* from Album *Creative Writing* (item 9); *Reshaping communities, changing expectations* from Album *Crime, Order and Social Control* (item 10); *Injustice and inequality* from Album *Earth in crisis: environmental policy in an international context* (item 11); *Exploring Psychology: Twin Studies 1* from Album *Exploring Psychology* by John Oates (item 12); *Concept of heritage* from Album *Heritage, whose heritage?* by Patrick Wright (item 13); *A day in the life of a hospital ward: Working in Teams* from Album *Introducing professional practice* (item 14); *Student Views of the OU* from Album *The Student Experience* (items 15, 16 and 17)

While every effort has been made to contact copyright holders, the Publishers apologize for any omissions, which they will be pleased to rectify at the earliest opportunity.

The Official Guide to PTE Academic Audio CD

Track	Item type	Page
Chapter 3		
2	Repeat sentence	42
3	Repeat sentence	45
4	Re-tell lecture	53
5	Re-tell lecture	56
6	Answer short question	58
7	Answer short question	60
Chapter 6		
8	Summarize spoken text	123
9	Summarize spoken text	126
10	Multiple-choice, choose multiple answers	129
11	Multiple-choice, choose multiple answers	132
12	Fill in the blanks	134
13	Fill in the blanks	136
14	Highlight correct summary	139
15	Highlight correct summary	142
16	Multiple-choice, choose single answer	144
17	Multiple-choice, choose single answer	147
18	Select missing word	149

Track	Item type	Page
19	Select missing word	151
20	Highlight incorrect words	153
21	Highlight incorrect words	156
22	Write from dictation	158
23	Write from dictation	160
Answer key		
24	Read aloud, sample response C1	172
25	Read aloud, sample response B2	172
26	Read aloud, sample response B1	172
27	Repeat sentence, sample response C1	172
28	Repeat sentence, sample response B2	173
29	Repeat sentence, sample response B1	173
30	Describe image, sample response C1	173
31	Describe image, sample response B2	173
32	Describe image, sample response B1	174
33	Re-tell lecture, sample response C1	174
34	Re-tell lecture, sample response B2	174
35	Re-tell lecture, sample response B1	175

The Official Guide to PTE Academic CD-ROM

Installing the software

To use the CD-ROM included with *The Official Guide to PTE Academic*, you must first install Adobe® Reader® 6 or above on your computer. You can download the software from the Internet.

Using the program

- Close all open applications, then insert the CD-ROM into the CD-ROM drive.
- The program will run automatically. You will see the main menu of the CD-ROM on screen.
- If the program does not run automatically, open "My computer" and double-click on the CD-ROM icon. Then click on the PTE icon to go to the main menu.
- Click on "Introduction" for an overview of the CD-ROM content and study hints.
- Click on "User manual" for a general outline of interface features and functionality, and instructions on operating the CD-ROM software.
- Click on "Item practice" to start the practice.
- Submit your responses to the items in a practice set to access the Answer key for the set.

System requirements
1024 x 768 screen resolution or above
32 million (32-bit) color display
Pentium 41.6GHz CPU or above
512MB RAM or above
32MB RAM or above XGA display card
16-bit Sound Blaster or compatible sound card
24x speed or higher CD-ROM drive
Headphones or speakers, built-in or external
Microphone, built-in or external

Supported operating systems
Microsoft® Windows® 2000 (SP4), XP (SP2) or
Windows® Vista
Mac OS X 10.4, 10.5 or 10.6; Recommended language: English

Software requirements
Adobe® Reader® 6 or above